BAKED DONUT COOKBOOK

Copyright © 2020 Holly Kristin

All Rights Reserved. No part of this book may be reproduced or used in any form or by any means without written permission from the author.

TABLE OF CONTENTS

Introduction 6

Chapter 1: Homemade Donut Basics 8

Chapter 2: Basic and Sugared Donuts 15

Easy Breakfast Donuts 15
Mini Donuts 18
Apple Donuts 21
Chocolate Coffee Donuts 24
Spiced Cake Donuts 27
Easy Sugared Donuts 30
Succulent Buttermilk Donuts 33
Apple Cider Donuts 36
Easy Pizza Donuts 39
Pineapple Donuts 42

Chapter 3: Glazed and Frosted Donuts 44

Chocolate Orange Donuts 44
Honey Glazed Donuts 48
Chocolate Banana Donuts 51
Sweet Potato Chocolate Donuts 54
Pink Funfetti Donuts 57
Maple Pumpkin Donuts 59
Banana Donuts with Chocolate Glaze 63
Buttermilk Pumpkin Donuts 66
Lemonade Cake Donuts 70
Red Velvet Donuts 72
Glazed Pumpkin Donuts 75
Vanilla Coconut Donuts 78
Chocolate Donuts 82

Creamy Glazed Donuts 85
Coconut Lime Donuts 88
Cream Donuts with Oreo 91
Lemon Poppy Seed Donuts 94
Fluffy Cake Donuts 97
Lemon Blueberry Donuts 100
Lemon Raspberry Donuts 103
Cookie and Cream Donuts 106
Apple Butter Donuts with Whole Wheat 110
Coffee Donuts 113

Chapter 4: Filled Donuts 116

Nutella-Filled Donut Muffins 116
Strawberry Jam Filled Donut Cupcakes 120
Peanut Butter Jelly Donuts 126
Jelly Donut Cupcakes 130
Cheesecake Stuffed Donuts 132
Strawberry Donuts 136
Cherries & Cream Filled Donuts 139
Apple Pie Donuts 143
Apricot Plum Donuts 147

Chapter 5: Donut Holes 151

Chocolate Cake Donut Holes 151
Cinnamon Donut Holes 155
Donut Holes with Vanilla Cream Glaze 158
Red Velvet Donut Holes 161
Nutella Filled Donut Holes 164
Moist Chocolate Donut Holes 167
Cream Cheese Donut Holes 170
Apple Cider Donut Holes 173
Pumpkin Donut Holes 176

Apple Cinnamon Donut Holes 179
Other Books by Holly Kristin 182

INTRODUCTION

Thank you for the purchase of *Baked Donut Cookbook: Easy and Delightful Donut Recipes to Make at Home without Fuss*. Donuts are the ultimate comfort food and they are a fun and easy treat that is perfect for any breakfast or brunch gathering.

Imagine the irresistible aroma from the oven and a little hint of jelly peeking out of the side of your donuts. Sugared, frosted, sprinkled, or filled donuts are sure to sweeten your day and satisfy your cravings anytime. It is so much fun to be able to make your own mouthwatering and mess-free donuts from scratch without leaving the comforts of your home.

Baked donuts are a healthier option compared to traditional deep-fried donuts and you can easily make them within 20 to 30 minutes. Baking donuts also help you cut down on prep, cleanup, and possible mess.

Making donuts at home can seem intimidating if you have never made them before. This cookbook shows you how easy it is to make donuts at home for significantly less than what it costs to purchase them. And the best part is that you do not need to stress with frying to create these classic, flavorful treats at home.

You will find delightful recipes and easy-to-follow instructions for making beautifully baked donuts, mini donuts, filled donuts, donut holes, and more inside this cookbook. So you don't experience any difficulty you may have encountered in the past with other donut recipes.

This ultimate cookbook provides you with the essential information you need to get started, including tips and tricks to keep your donuts fresh for weeks. With more than 50 delightfully simple recipes, helpful instructions, and nutritional information included, you are sure to succeed with *Baked Donut Cookbook*, regardless of your skill level. Enjoy!

CHAPTER 1: HOMEMADE DONUT BASICS

Making homemade donuts is undoubtedly much easier than you think, and it doesn't require any special equipment or ingredients. For instance, if you don't have a donut cutter, simply make use of your cookie cutters or juice glasses. The following is an overview of necessary equipment and ingredients for baking your donuts;

BASIC EQUIPMENT

For donut making at home, you probably already own the few pieces of equipment needed. In addition to the simple kitchen tools like bowls for mixing the ingredients, you should get the following tools before getting started.

1. Kitchen Scale: This is not essential, but it makes it super-easy to measure ingredients such as flour and sugar steadily. Flour tends to compress when you measure in cups, resulting in excess flour being used in the batter. Using a kitchen scale also makes it easier to double or halve a recipe.

2. Stand Mixer with Dough Hook and Paddle Attachment: While you can surely make donuts without a stand mixer, the one with a dough hook helps to activate the gluten while kneading the dough. It also decreases the possibility of using too much flour in your dough. If you don't have a stand mixer, you can make use of a hand mixer or simply use your hand to mix until blended.

3. Pastry or Piping Bag: You can use a pastry bag fitted with a half-inch circular tip to make round-bottom donuts. A star-shaped tip can be used to make ridged crullers. If you don't have a pastry or piping bag, simply cut off the corner of a resealable plastic bag to fill your donut pan.

4. Donut Cutter: This tool makes it easy to punch out many raised donuts within a few minutes. When purchasing, choose the donut cutter made of stiff metal and with a detachable middle punch for easy cleaning. If you can't purchase a donut cutter, use a cookie cutter or juice glass to cut out rounds of donuts and use your finger to punch a hole in the middle of the round.

5. Donut Pans: These pans are essential to make classic round-bottom donuts. Donut pans are made of silicone or metal. You can use a mini-muffin pan to create your donuts if you don't have a donut pan. However, the donuts will not have typical round shapes.

6. Doughnut Machine: This appliance offers an easier way to create donuts at home. It helps to cook the whole donut with contact heat so that the top and bottom of your donuts have the same outside texture.

ESSENTIAL INGREDIENTS

You can make donuts at home with the simplest of pantry staples like flour, butter, yeast, sugar, baking soda, baking powder, and oil for frying. Here is an overview of the necessary ingredients for making donuts at home.

1. Flour: All-purpose flour is great for cake donuts, which doesn't require gluten expansion like raised donuts, and are likely to become a bit tough with bread flour. On the other hand, raised or yeast donuts benefit from higher-protein bread flour because it makes the dough more elastic and helps to produce the lightest of pastries.

2. Baking Soda and Baking Powder: They are used to create a rise in baked donuts. Baking soda is more potent than baking powder, but it needs an acid to actuate it. Recipes that use baking soda will include ingredients like buttermilk or sour cream to make the donuts puff up.

3. Yeast: Yeast is usually used in making raised donuts. You can use active-dry or instant yeast, depending on what the recipe specifies. If you are a regular baker, it is advisable to skip the small envelopes of yeast and purchase yours in a larger quantity. You can store the yeast for up to 6 months in the refrigerator.

4. Sugar: While you can use granulated sugar in your donut recipes, superfine sugar works perfectly as a fantastic donut-coating alternative to glazes and blends more quickly into the dry ingredients. Light or dark brown sugar or darker sugars like muscovado are great for baked donuts.

5. Butter, Oil, and Other Fats: Aside from the oil used for deep-frying, donuts require a bit of fat in their batter or dough to create fluffy and soft donuts. Solid fats such as butter, lard, or coconut oil are much better than liquid fats.

KEEPING YOUR DONUTS FRESH

It is almost impossible to have leftover donuts, but if you do, it is essential to store them properly to enjoy a fresh, delicious treat another day. Donuts can spoil quickly or go stale because they contain fat, butter, and sugar. Check out the following tips on storing your donuts to keep them fresh for some days.

1. Storing at room temperature

Put your leftover donuts in an airtight container or storage bag. Make sure that the container or storage bag is sealed tightly so that your donuts don't become stale. Keeping your donuts out of direct sunlight will make them last longer.

If you want to consume the donuts within one to two days, you store them at room temperature. But if the donuts are filled with cream, you will need to refrigerate them to prevent spoilage.

When you are ready to eat the stored donuts, put them on a heat-resistant plate, place in the microwave, and warm for about five seconds to freshen them up. Avoid microwaving the donuts for too long so that they don't become stiff and the glaze or frosting doesn't melt away.

2. Storing in the refrigerator

Put your leftover donuts in an airtight container or storage bag and place in the fridge for up to one week. You should note that any glaze or icing on the donuts would become runny in the refrigerator. Although it won't affect the freshness, it's best to consume any donut with glaze or icing sooner.

When you are ready to eat your refrigerated donuts, microwave them at 15-second intervals. Microwaving them can bring back moisture to the chilled donuts and really freshen them. However, note that the icing or glaze on the donuts may melt slightly in the microwave.

3. Freezing unfrosted donuts

Plain and powdered donuts freeze perfectly. But icing and glazed donuts will become messy when thawed.

Freeze your leftover donuts after putting them in an airtight container and laying them with wax paper. This will prevent them from sticking together in the freezer; so that, if you want to eat one donut, you won't need to thaw the entire container before taking out a donut.

Make sure you put the container inside a sealed, heavy-duty freezer bag to prevent ice crystals from developing inside the sealed container. You can freeze the donuts for up to two to three months.

When you are ready to eat your frozen donuts, place them on a plate and leave them uncovered on the counter for about fifteen minutes to thaw them; the donuts will become soggy if you cover them. After fifteen minutes, microwave the donuts at 15-second intervals to make them moist and nice again.

CHAPTER 2: BASIC AND SUGARED DONUTS

EASY BREAKFAST DONUTS

This donut recipe will make you a delicious breakfast treat. You can shape the donuts as you prefer.

Total Time: 30 minutes

Yield: 12 serving

Ingredients

- 1/2 cup of butter, melted
- 1 tbsp honey
- 3 large eggs
- 1 cup of buttermilk
- 3 cups of all-purpose flour
- 2 tsp ground cinnamon

- 1/2 tsp ground cloves
- 1 tsp ground nutmeg
- 1 tsp baking soda
- 2 tsp baking powder
- 1 cup of white sugar

Directions

- Preheat your oven to 400°F.
- Grease a donut pan lightly.
- Mix up the dry ingredients in a bowl.
- In a different bowl, mix up butter, honey, eggs, and buttermilk. And then, add to the flour mixture and mix thoroughly.
- Scoop the mixture into the cavity of the donut pan.
- Place the pan inside the oven and bake until donut spring back when pressed lightly, about 12 minutes.

Nutrition Information Per Serving

280 calories; sodium 259.2mg 10% DV; cholesterol 67.7mg 23% DV; fat 9.5g 15% DV; carbohydrates 43.7g 14% DV; protein 5.6g 11% DV.

MINI DONUTS

This is a fantastic recipe for delectable mini donuts without frying. These delightful donuts have the consistency of cake donuts and are very addicting.

Total Time: 30 minutes

Yield: 36 mini donuts

Ingredients

Donuts:

- 1 egg, large
- 1/3 cup of white sugar
- 5 tbsp softened butter
- 1/2 tsp vanilla extract
- 1/4 cup of milk
- 1/8 tsp salt
- 1/4 tsp ground nutmeg, or more to taste
- 1/2 tsp baking powder

- 2/3 cup of all-purpose flour

Coating:

- 1 tsp ground cinnamon
- 1/3 cup of white sugar

Directions

- Preheat your oven to 350°F.
- Coat small muffin cups with cooking spray or line them with paper liners.
- Mix up flour, salt, nutmeg, and baking powder in a bowl. Combine vanilla extract and milk in a separate container.
- In a third bowl, mix up 1/3 cup of white sugar and butter with an electric mixer until creamy and smooth, then stir in the egg.
- Combine the flour mix with the milk mix and butter mix. Mix up the batter until smooth. Scoop the mixture into a piping bag and pipe into the muffin cups up to 2/3 full.

- Place the muffin cups in the oven and bake for about 10 to 12 minutes or until the donuts spring back when pressed lightly.

- Combine cinnamon and 1/3 cup of white sugar in a container. Add in warm donuts and toss gently with your hands to coat.

Nutrition Information Per Serving

161 calories; sodium 115.6mg 5% DV; cholesterol 38.2mg 13% DV; fat 7.2g 11% DV; carbohydrates 22.6g 7% DV; protein 2g 4% DV.

APPLE DONUTS

This easy donut recipe will make you delicious tender donuts dotted with tart apple pieces. You coat the batter with sufficient cinnamon sugar mix and bake them.

Total Time: 35 minutes

Yield: 24 mini donuts

Ingredients

Donuts:

- 2 large eggs, whisked
- 1 cup of milk
- 2 cups of chopped apples
- 1/2 cup of vegetable shortening
- 1 tsp ground cinnamon
- 1 tsp ground nutmeg
- 1 tsp salt
- 1 tbsp baking powder

- 1 cup of white sugar
- 3 cups of all-purpose flour

Coating:

- 2 tsp ground cinnamon
- 1 cup of sugar
- 1/2 cup of butter, melted

Directions

- Preheat your oven to 350°F.
- Coat 2 (12-cavity) mini donut pans with cooking spray.
- In a big bowl, mix up flour, cinnamon, nutmeg, salt, baking powder, and sugar. Mix thoroughly using a fork until blended.
- Add in the vegetable shortening and mix with the fork until the mixture is broken up into small clumps.
- In a separate bowl, combine eggs, milk, and apples; stir into the flour mixture and mix until combined.
- Scoop the mixture into the prepared donut pans and

place in the oven.

- Bake donuts for about ten minutes or until slightly browned on the bottoms. Transfer the donuts to a wire rack to cool.

- In the meantime, place the melted butter for topping in a bowl. In a separate bowl, combine 2 tsp cinnamon and 1 cup of sugar.

- Dip the donuts into the butter and then into the cinnamon-sugar mix to coat. Enjoy!

Note: If you want to make muffins, scoop the dough into greased muffin pans and bake at 350°F for about 20 to 25 minutes or until the tops spring back when pressed lightly.

Nutrition Information Per Serving

211 calories; sodium 176.6mg 7% DV; cholesterol 26.5mg 9% DV; fat 8.9g 14% DV; carbohydrates 30.9g 10% DV; protein 2.6g 5% DV.

CHOCOLATE COFFEE DONUTS

This chocolate coffee donut recipe will make you baked donuts with amazing flavor and texture. You can use your favorite glaze or powdered sugar.

Total Time: 35 minutes

Yield: 6 donuts

Ingredients

- 1/4 cup of chocolate chips, or to taste
- 1/2 tsp vanilla extract
- 1 tablespoon unsalted butter
- 1 large egg
- 1/4 cup of strong brewed coffee
- 1/4 cup plus 2 tbsp buttermilk
- 1/2 cup of packed brown sugar
- 1 tsp baking powder
- 1/4 cup of cocoa powder, unsweetened

- 1 cup of all-purpose flour
- 1 tsp butter, unsalted

Directions

- Preheat your oven to 400°F.
- Coat a 6-cavity donut pan with one teaspoon of butter.
- In a big bowl, mix up flour, baking powder, and cocoa powder.
- In a separate bowl, whisk together brown sugar, vanilla extract, one tbsp butter, egg, coffee, and buttermilk. Add the wet ingredients to the flour mixture and mix thoroughly. Add the chocolate chips and stir to combine.
- Scoop the batter into a big plastic bag and cut off 1 corner. Squeeze the mixture into the greased donut pan and fill each cup to 2/3 full.
- Place the pan in the oven and bake for 8 minutes or until the donuts spring back when pressed lightly.
- Remove from the oven and allow cooling in the pan on a wire rack for about five minutes. Turn over the pan

directly on the wire rack to get the donuts out. Allow cooling for five minutes. Enjoy them warm.

Nutrition Information Per Serving

229 calories; sodium 116.6mg 5% DV; cholesterol 38.4mg 13% DV; fat 6.3g 10% DV; carbohydrates 41.3g 13% DV; protein 4.8g 10% DV.

SPICED CAKE DONUTS

This is a delectably moist and healthy version of cake donuts with plenty of spiced flavors.

Total Time: 45 minutes

Yield: 12 donuts

Ingredients

Donuts:

- 2 tsp vanilla extract
- 1 large egg, whisked lightly
- 2 tbsp butter, melted
- 1 cup of apple cider vinegar
- 1 cup of applesauce
- 1/2 tsp kosher salt
- 1/2 tsp pumpkin pie spice
- 1 tsp ground cinnamon
- 2 tsp baking powder

- 1 1/4 cups of white sugar
- 2 cups of all-purpose flour

Coating:

- 4 tbsp melted unsalted butter
- ½ tsp ground cinnamon
- ½ cup of white sugar

Directions

- Preheat your oven to 325°F.
- Spray a 12-cup donut pan with cooking spray
- In a big bowl, combine all the dry ingredients.
- In a different bowl, mix together applesauce, vanilla extract, egg, melted butter, and apple cider vinegar.
- Combine the wet ingredients with the flour mixture and mix until just combined.
- Scoop the mixture into the donut pan and fill each cavity to ¾ full.
- Place the donut pan inside the preheated oven and bake

for about 17 minutes or until a toothpick inserted at the middle comes out clean.

- Remove the pan from the oven and allow cooling for five minutes before moving the donuts to a baking sheet.

- Mix up cinnamon and sugar in a bowl. Dip warm donuts into the melted butter and then dip into the cinnamon-sugar mix. Enjoy your donuts warm!

Nutrition Information Per Serving

270 calories; sodium 172.1mg 7% DV; cholesterol 33.2mg 11% DV; fat 6.5g 10% DV; carbohydrates 50.7g 16% DV; protein 2.9g 6% DV.

EASY SUGARED DONUTS

This is an easy donut recipe that you can enjoy at any time of the day.

Total Time: 45 minutes

Yield: 8 donuts

Ingredients

Donuts:

- 1 ½ tsp pure vanilla extract
- 2 tbsp melted butter, unsalted
- ¼ cup of yogurt
- ¼ cup of milk
- ⅓ cup of packed light brown sugar
- 1 large egg
- ¼ tsp ground nutmeg
- ½ tsp ground cinnamon
- ½ tsp salt

- ¼ tsp baking soda
- 1 tsp baking powder
- 1 cup of all-purpose flour

Topping:

- ½ cup of unsalted butter, melted
- 1 tsp ground cinnamon
- 1 cup of granulated sugar

Directions

- Preheat your oven to 375°F.
- Coat a donut pan with baking spray and set aside.
- In a big bowl, mix up flour, nutmeg, cinnamon, salt, baking soda, and baking powder.
- In a separate bowl, whisk together yogurt, milk, brown sugar, and egg until smooth. Stir in vanilla and melted butter and keep whisking until well combined.
- Pour the dry ingredients into the flour mixture and mix until blended. Avoid over mixing.

- Scoop the donut into the donut cavities (it is recommended that you use a big zipped-top bag for ease by cutting off a corner of the bag's bottom and piping the dough into each donut cup, filling up to ⅔ to ¾ full).

- Bake until the edges are browned lightly, about 9 to 10 minutes.

- Allow cooling for about 5 minutes, then place on a wire rack. Let donut cool completely.

- To coat the donuts, combine cinnamon and sugar in a bowl. Dip the donuts into the melted butter and then into the sugar mix to coat all sides.

- Serve the donuts immediately.

SUCCULENT BUTTERMILK DONUTS

These yummy donuts are soft and airy on the inside and crispy on the outside. You can toss them in a sugar-cinnamon mixture, glaze them with chocolate frosting, or glaze them with powdered sugar-water icing. Enjoy!

Total Time: 60 minutes

Yield: 12 donuts

Ingredients

Donuts:

- 4 tbsp melted vegetable shortening
- 1 tsp vanilla extract, pure
- 1 tsp baking soda
- 2 large eggs
- 1 cup of buttermilk
- 1/2 tsp salt
- 1 tsp freshly grated nutmeg

- 1 tsp baking powder

- 2 tbsp cornstarch

- 1 cup of white sugar

- 2 cups of all-purpose flour

Coating:

- 1 cup of sifted powdered sugar

Directions

- Preheat your oven to 375°F.

- Set the oven rack to the upper-middle position. Then, coat a donut pan with the cooking spray.

- In a big bowl, combine flour, salt, nutmeg, baking powder, cornstarch, and sugar.

- Mix up vanilla extract, baking soda, eggs, and buttermilk in a small bowl.

- Add the melted and cooled shortening to the flour mix and combine until blended.

- Add the buttermilk mixture and mix thoroughly.

Allow the batter to sit for ten to fifteen minutes.

- Scoop the mixture into the cups of the coated donut pan up to 2/3 full.

- Place the donuts on the upper-middle rack in the oven and bake for 12 to 15 minutes or until golden brown.

- Remove the donuts from the oven and allow cooling inside the pan for five minutes before transferring to a wire rack.

- Put powdered sugar in a small paper bag and toss the donuts in the sugar to coat.

- Repeat the process for the remaining batter.

Nutrition Information Per Serving

247 calories; sodium 276.2mg 11% DV; cholesterol 31.8mg 11% DV; fat 5.6g 9% DV; carbohydrates 45.5g 15% DV; protein 3.9g 8% DV.

APPLE CIDER DONUTS

These easy baked donuts are moist, fluffy, and delicious. You coat them generously with a spiced sugar coating.

Total Time: 40 minutes

Yield: 10 -12 donuts

Ingredients

Donuts:

- 1 tsp vanilla extract
- ¼ cup of vegetable oil
- ½ cup of buttermilk
- ½ cup of light brown sugar
- 1 egg, large
- ¼ tsp ground nutmeg
- ½ tsp ground cloves
- 1 tsp ground cinnamon
- ¼ tsp salt

- 1 tsp baking powder
- 2 cups of all-purpose flour
- 1 cup of apple cider vinegar

Coating:

- 6 tbsp melted unsalted butter
- ¼ tsp ground nutmeg
- ½ tsp ground cloves
- 1 tsp ground cinnamon
- 1 cup of granulated sugar

Directions

- Simmer apple cider vinegar in a pan over low heat until reduced to a half cup. Stir occasionally. Let in cool for 10 to 15 minutes.
- Preheat your oven to 350°F. Coat a donut pan with cooking spray.
- In a bowl, combine flour, spices, salt, and baking powder.

- In a separate bowl, mix up buttermilk, vanilla, and apple cider vinegar until smooth.

- Combine the wet ingredients with the flour mixture. Mix until just combined.

- Scoop the mixture into the cups on the donut pan, filling up to 2/3 full.

- Bake donuts in the oven until a toothpick inserted in the middle comes out clean, about 10 to 12 minutes.

- Remove from the oven and allow cooling for 5 minutes. Remove from the pan and set on a wire rack.

- Combine sugar, cinnamon, cloves, and nutmeg. Dip warm donuts into the melted butter and coat with the spiced sugar mix.

Nutrition Information Per Serving

286 calories; sodium 115mg; cholesterol 31mg; fat 11g; carbohydrates 44g; protein 3g; sugar 27g.

EASY PIZZA DONUTS

Total Time: 15 minutes

Yield: 8 donuts

Ingredients

- 3/4 cup of cold buttermilk
- 1/2 cup of butter, room temperature
- 1 teaspoon salt
- 1 tablespoon baking powder
- 1 tablespoon sugar
- 2 cups of all-purpose flour
- ½ to 1 cup of shredded cheese
- 1 teaspoon Italian seasoning
- ½ cup of tomato sauce
- ½ cup of your favorite pizza toppings

Directions

- Preheat your oven to 375ºF.

- Coat a donut pan with cooking spray.

- Combine flour, salt, baking powder, and sugar in a big bowl. Add butter and buttermilk and mix until well combined.

- Sprinkle flour lightly on a surface to roll out your dough. Roll the dough into 1-inch thick rectangular.

- Using a donut cutter, cut out the donuts and set aside.

- Combine the tomato sauce with the Italian seasoning in a bowl and spread one tablespoon of the mixture on each donut.

- Sprinkle the donuts with the shredded cheese and garnish with your favorite pizza toppings.

- Bake in the oven until a toothpick inserted at the center comes out clean, and the outside is lightly golden brown, about 10 to 15 minutes.

- Remove the donut from the oven and allow cooling for three to five minutes in the pan before removing from the pan.

Nutrition Information Per Serving

357 calories; sodium 972mg; cholesterol 50mg; fat 19g; carbohydrates 37g; protein 10g; sugar 4g.

PINEAPPLE DONUTS

These amazing pineapple donuts would be flipped upside down when done. Enjoy!

Total Time: 30 minutes

Yield: 4 - 5 donuts

Ingredients

- 1 cup of self-rising flour
- 1 ½ tsp pure vanilla extract
- 2 tbsp melted unsalted butter
- ¼ cup of sour cream
- 2 tbsp fresh pineapple juice
- 2 tbsp whole milk
- ⅓ cup of light brown sugar (add extra for sprinkling)
- 1 egg, large
- Maraschino cherries for topping
- 1 (15 oz.) can pineapple rings

Directions

- Preheat your oven to 350ºF.

- Coat a donut pan with cooking spray.

- Combine brown sugar, egg, vanilla extract, melted butter, sour cream, pineapple juice, and milk in a bowl. Mix until smooth, and then stir in the self-rising flour.

- Once the ingredients are combined, slice the pineapple rings in half lengthwise to ensure an even ratio of the fruit and dough.

- Add one tablespoon of brown sugar to each cavity of the donut pan and place a pineapple ring on the brown sugar. Scoop and spread the batter evenly over the pineapple rings.

- Bake in the oven for 15 to 20 minutes. Remove from the oven and allow cooling.

- Carefully turn the donut pan upside side to get the donuts out. Place a Maraschino cherry in the center of each donut.

CHAPTER 3: GLAZED AND FROSTED DONUTS

CHOCOLATE ORANGE DONUTS

These easy baked donuts are moist, fluffy, and delicious. You infuse with orange and top them with orange ganache. Enjoy!

Total Time: 30 minutes

Yield: 12 donuts

Ingredients

Donuts:

- 2 tbsp melted unsalted butter
- ½ cup of Greek yogurt
- ½ cup of light brown sugar
- 1 egg, large
- ¼ cup of orange juice

- 1 large orange zest
- ¼ tsp ground nutmeg
- ¼ tsp salt
- ½ cup of cocoa powder
- ¼ tsp baking soda
- 2 tsp baking powder
- 1 ½ cups of all-purpose flour

Glaze:

- 2 tsp orange juice
- 2 tsp light corn syrup or golden syrup
- 2 tablespoons unsalted butter
- ½ cup of chocolate chips
- Chocolate sprinkles, to garnish

Directions

- Preheat your oven to 350°F.
- Coat 2 donut pans with cooking spray.

- Combine flour, zest, nutmeg, salt, cocoa powder, baking soda, and baking powder in a bowl.

- Mix melted butter, yogurt, sugar, egg, and orange juice in a separate bowl until smooth.

- Combine the wet ingredients with the flour mixture. Mix till just combined. Fold the blueberries into the mixture and allow them to break up while mixing.

- Scoop the mixture into the cups on the donut pan, filling up to 2/3 full.

- Bake donuts in the oven until a toothpick inserted in the middle comes out clean, about 7 to 10 minutes.

- Remove from the oven and allow cooling for 5 minutes. Remove from the pan and set on a wire rack.

- Place a parchment paper beneath the wire rack.

- Make the glaze; place syrup, butter, and chocolate chips into a microwave bowl. Microwave the mixture until melted and smooth, stirring frequently. Add orange juice and stir. Remove from the microwave.

- Dip warm donuts into the glaze and place on the wire rack to set. Top with chocolate sprinkles.

Nutrition Information Per Serving

199 calories; sodium 179mg; cholesterol 27mg; fat 7g; carbohydrates 31g; protein 4g; sugar 18g.

HONEY GLAZED DONUTS

This is an easy recipe for delicious honey glazed donuts. They are so warm and moist inside.

Total Time: 25 minutes

Yield: 15 donuts

Ingredients

Donuts:

- ½ teaspoon nutmeg
- ½ teaspoon cinnamon
- 1 ½ cup of milk
- ¾ cup of brown sugar
- ½ cup of butter, melted
- ¾ teaspoon salt
- 2 large eggs, beaten
- 2 teaspoons baking powder
- ⅓ cup of cornstarch

- 2 cups of flour

Glaze:

- ½ tablespoon lemon juice
- 3 tbsp honey

Directions

- Preheat your oven to 350°F.
- Coat 2 donut pans with cooking spray.
- Combine flour, cornstarch, salt, and baking powder in a bowl.
- In a separate bowl, mix eggs, butter, nutmeg, cinnamon, and brown sugar until smooth.
- Combine the wet ingredients with the flour mixture and mix until just combined.
- Scoop the mixture into the cups on the donut pan, filling up to 2/3 full.
- Bake donuts in the oven until a toothpick inserted in the middle comes out clean, about 12 to 15 minutes.

- Remove from the oven and allow cooling for 5 minutes.

- Remove from the pan and set on a wire rack. Place a parchment paper beneath the wire rack.

- Combine honey and lemon juice in a bowl and dip warm donuts into the glaze to coat.

Nutrition Information Per Serving

207 calories; sodium 195mg; cholesterol 40mg; fat 7g; carbohydrates 31g; protein 3g; sugar 15g

CHOCOLATE BANANA DONUTS

Total Time: 30 minutes

Yield: 12 donuts

Ingredients

Banana Bread Donuts:

- 1/4 tsp salt
- 1 tsp vanilla extract
- 3/4 tsp baking soda
- 1 cup of mashed banana
- 1/4 cup of unsalted butter, melted
- 1/4 cup of dark chocolate, diced into chunks
- 2 tbsp raw honey
- 4 eggs, large
- 1/4 cup of shredded coconut, unsweetened
- 1/4 cup + 2 tbsp coconut flour
- 1/4 cup + 2 tbsp almond flour

Chocolate Glaze:

- 1 tbsp non-dairy milk
- 1 1/2 tbsp coconut oil
- 2 tbsp raw honey
- 5 tbsp cocoa powder

Optional Toppings:

- 1 medium banana, sliced
- 1 to 2 tbsp dark chocolate, chopped finely
- 1/4 cup of shredded coconut, unsweetened (toasted in a pan for two min.)

Directions

- Preheat your oven to 350ºF.
- Coat 2 (6-cavity) donut pans with cooking spray.
- Combine flours, salt, baking soda, and shredded coconut in a bowl.
- In a separate bowl, mix up mashed banana, vanilla, melted butter, honey, and eggs. Mix until smooth.

- Add the wet ingredients to the flour mixture and mix until combined. Stir in chocolate chunks.

- Scoop the mixture into the donut pan and fill each cavity to ¾ full.

- Place the donut pan inside the preheated oven and bake until a toothpick inserted at the middle comes out clean, about eight to ten to twelve minutes.

- Remove the pan from the oven and allow cooling for five minutes before removing the donuts to a wire rack.

- To make your chocolate glaze, place coconut oil and honey in a small saucepan and melt over low heat. Pour the mixture into a bowl and mix with non-dairy milk and cocoa powder until thick and smooth.

- Refrigerate the glaze for a few minutes to thicken it.

- Then, toast shredded coconut for two minutes in a pan, if using.

- Dip each donut's top in the glaze and top with toasted coconut, sliced banana, or dark chocolate.

SWEET POTATO CHOCOLATE DONUTS

These healthy chocolate glazed donuts are made with sweet potato instead of flour! This easy donut recipe is gluten-free and great for celebrations. Enjoy!

Total Time: 30 minutes

Yield: 7 donuts

Ingredients

Donut:

- ¼ tsp baking soda
- ¼ tsp baking powder
- ½ tsp sea salt
- 2 tbsp arrowroot flour
- 2 tbsp coconut flour
- 2 tbsp maple syrup
- ¼ cup of coconut sugar
- ¼ cup of black cocoa powder (you may use regular

- cocoa powder)
- 3 tbsp coconut oil
- 2 eggs, large
- 1 small raw white sweet potato (mince in a blender or food processor)

Glaze:

- ¼ tsp sea salt
- ¼ cup of coconut oil
- 1 cup of chocolate chips

Directions

- Preheat your oven to 350ºF.
- Coat a donut pan with coconut oil.
- Place all the donut ingredients in a blender or food processor and process until smooth.
- Pour the batter into a plastic bag and pipe into the cavities of the donut pan.
- Bake the donuts in the oven until a toothpick inserted

at the middle comes out clean, about 15 to 18 minutes.

- Remove from the oven and allow slight cooling before transferring to a wire rack.

- Place the glaze ingredients in a small pan and melt over low heat, stirring frequently.

- Allow slight cooling of the glaze to thicken before dipping the donuts in it.

Nutrition Information Per Serving

353 calories; sodium 284mg 12% DV; cholesterol 27mg 9% DV; fat 21g 32% DV; carbohydrates 41g 14% DV; protein 7g 14% DV; sugars 23g.

PINK FUNFETTI DONUTS

Total Time: 25 minutes

Yield: 15 donuts

Ingredients

- ½ teaspoon red food color
- 2 tablespoons melted butter
- 2 large eggs, beaten
- 1 ¼ tablespoons cocoa powder
- ¾ cups of buttermilk
- 1 teaspoon pure vanilla extract
- 2 teaspoons baking powder
- ½ teaspoon salt
- ¾ cups of granulated sugar
- 2 cups of all-purpose flour

Directions

- Preheat your oven to 350°F.

- Coat donut pans with cooking spray.

- Combine flour, baking powder, salt, and sugar in a bowl.

- In a separate bowl, mix buttermilk, vanilla, butter, and eggs until smooth.

- Combine the wet ingredients with the flour mixture and mix until blended.

- Add the food color and cocoa powder to the batter and mix until just combined.

- Scoop the mixture into the cups on the donut pan, filling up to 2/3 full.

- Bake donuts in the oven until a toothpick inserted in the middle comes out clean, about 8 to 10 minutes. You can also bake the donuts in a mini-donut maker for three to five minutes.

- Remove from the oven and allow cooling for 5 minutes. Remove from the pan and set on a wire rack.

- Dip warm donuts in your favorite glaze and sprinkle funfetti over the donuts before the glaze dries.

MAPLE PUMPKIN DONUTS

This baked pumpkin donut recipe is terrific. You dip the donuts in maple glaze and sprinkle with finely dices pumpkin seeds.

Total Time: 50 minutes

Yield: 8 serving

Ingredients

Donuts:

- 1 egg
- 1/4 cup of buttermilk
- 1/3 cup of maple syrup
- 1/3 cup of vegetable oil
- 3/4 cup of pumpkin puree
- 1/4 cup of light brown sugar
- 1/8 tsp ground cloves
- 1/4 tsp salt

- 1/4 tsp ground allspice
- 1/4 tsp ground nutmeg
- 1/2 tsp ground ginger
- 3/4 tsp ground cinnamon
- 1 tsp baking powder
- 1 cup of all-purpose flour
- 1 tsp vegetable oil, or as needed

Glaze:

- 1/4 cup of finely diced pumpkin seeds, roasted
- 3 tbsp maple syrup
- 1/2 cup od confectioners' sugar

Directions

- Preheat your oven to 375°F.
- Coat a donut pan with one teaspoon of vegetable oil.
- In a big bowl, combine flour, cloves, salt, allspice, nutmeg, ginger, cinnamon, and baking powder. Add

brown sugar to mix well to incorporate the ingredients.

- In a separate bowl, whisk together pumpkin puree, egg, buttermilk, 1/3 cup maple syrup, and 1/3 cup vegetable oil.

- Add the wet ingredients to the flour mixture and mix until just combined. Place in the refrigerator to sit for 20 to 40 minutes.

- Scoop the mixture into the cups on the donut pan, filling up to 2/3 full.

- Bake donuts in the oven for 9 to 13 minutes or until a toothpick inserted in the middle comes out clean.

- Remove from the oven and allow cooling for 5 minutes. Using a small knife or spatula, loosen the donuts' edges and set them on a wire rack.

- In a small bowl, mix up 3 tablespoons of maple syrup and confectioners' sugar.

- Coat your donut in the glaze and place on the wire rack to set for about two to three minutes.

- Sprinkle pumpkin seeds over the glazed donuts.

Note: To make a thinner consistency of the glaze, simply add a little water (about ¼ teaspoon). Stir to blend the mixture.

Nutrition Information Per Serving

275 calories; sodium 209.8mg 8% DV; cholesterol 23.6mg 8% DV; fat 11.1g 17% DV; carbohydrates 41.9g 14% DV; protein 3.3g 7% DV.

BANANA DONUTS WITH CHOCOLATE GLAZE

These delightful banana donuts are baked and coated with dark chocolate glaze.

Total Time: 40 minutes

Yield: 8-9 donuts

Ingredients

Donuts:

- 2 tbsp buttermilk or whole milk
- ½ tsp vanilla extract
- ½ cup of mashed banana (one medium banana)
- ¼ cup of unsalted butter, melted
- ⅓ cup of packed dark or light brown sugar
- 1 egg, large
- ¼ tsp ground nutmeg
- ½ tsp ground cinnamon
- ½ tsp salt

- ¼ tsp baking soda
- 1 tsp baking powder
- 1 cup of all-purpose flour

Dark Chocolate Glaze

- 2 tsp water
- 2 tsp light corn syrup
- 2 tbsp butter, melted
- ½ cup of dark chocolate chips

Directions

- Preheat your oven to 375°F.
- Coat a donut pan with baking spray.
- In a big bowl, combine flour, nutmeg, cinnamon, salt, baking soda, and baking powder.
- In a different bowl, whisk together egg and brown sugar. Stir in buttermilk, vanilla, mashed banana, and butter. Mix until smooth.

- Add the wet ingredients to the flour mixture and mix until just combined. Avoid overmixing.

- Scoop the mixture into the cups on the donut pan, filling up to 2/3 full.

- Bake donuts in the oven for 9 to 12 minutes.

- Remove from the oven and allow cooling for 5 minutes. Set on a wire rack and place a parchment paper beneath the wire rack.

- Make your dark chocolate glaze by combining water, corn syrup, melted butter, and chocolate chips in a microwave bowl. Place inside the microwave and melt in 20 seconds intervals, frequently stirring, until fully melted.

- Dip the top of the warm donuts into the glaze and serve warm.

BUTTERMILK PUMPKIN DONUTS

These maple-glazed donuts are so delicious. You will enjoy them

Total Time: 45 minutes

Yield: 12 donuts

Ingredients

Donuts:

- 1 tsp vanilla extract
- 1 cup of pumpkin puree
- 1 egg yolk
- 1 egg
- 1/3 cup of buttermilk
- 1/4 cup of vegetable oil
- 1/2 stick butter, melted
- 1 cup of packed dark brown sugar
- 1/2 tsp of salt

- 1/4 tsp of baking soda

- 1 ½ tsp of baking powder

- 2 tsp of pumpkin pie spice

- 1 ½ cups of all-purpose flour

Glaze:

- 1/2 cup of coarsely chopped pecans (optional)

- 1/2 tsp of vanilla extract

- 1 cup of confectioners' sugar

- 2 tbsp of pure maple syrup

- 2 tbsp of cream or milk

- 1/2 cup of packed dark brown sugar

- 1/4 cup of butter

Directions

- Preheat your oven to 350°F.

- Coat two 6-cup donut pans with cooking spray.

- In a bowl, combine flour, salt, baking soda, baking

powder, and pumpkin pie spice.

- In a separate bowl, mix up brown sugar, vanilla, pumpkin puree, egg yolk, whole egg, buttermilk, oil, and butter until smooth.

- Combine the wet ingredients with the flour mixture and mix until blended.

- Scoop the mixture into the prepared donut pans and bake in the oven for 15 to 18 minutes or until the donut spring back when pressed lightly.

- Remove from the oven and transfer the donuts to a wire rack to cool while you make the glaze.

- Melt butter in a saucepan over low heat until completely melted. Remove the melted butter from the heat and stir in maple syrup, cream/milk, and brown sugar.

- Cook the mixture over low heat for 30 seconds or until bubbly. Remove the pan from the heat and add in vanilla and powdered sugar. Mix until smooth.

- Coat the donuts with the glaze and sprinkle pecans on

the donuts, if desired.

- Allow the glaze to set for about 15 minutes.

Nutrition Information Per Serving

382 calories; sodium 284.2mg 11% DV; cholesterol 56.6mg 19% DV; fat 17.5g 27% DV; carbohydrates 54.7g 18% DV; protein 3.4g 7% DV.

LEMONADE CAKE DONUTS

Total Time: 25 minutes

Yield: 10 donuts

Ingredients

Donuts:

- 2 large eggs
- 2 tablespoons melted butter
- 3/4 cup of buttermilk
- 2 ¾ cups of lemon-flavored box cake mix
- pink food coloring (optional)

Glaze:

- 1 teaspoon lemon extract (you can use vanilla/orange/almond)
- 3 tablespoons whole milk
- 1 cup of powdered sugar

Directions

- Preheat your oven to 350°F.

- Coat donut pans with cooking spray.

- Combine all the ingredients in a big bowl and mix until just combined.

- Scoop the mixture into the cups on the donut pan, filling up to 2/3 full.

- Bake donuts in the oven until a toothpick inserted in the middle comes out clean, about 8 to 10 minutes.

- Remove from the oven and allow cooling for 5 minutes. Remove from the pan and set on a wire rack.

- Make the glaze by mixing all the glaze ingredients in a bowl.

- Dip warm donuts into the glaze and set on the wire rack. If using, add sprinkles immediately after dipping into the glaze.

RED VELVET DONUTS

These delightful red velvet donuts are topped with cream cheese icing and are so easy to make. Enjoy!

Total Time: 20 minutes

Yield: 6 donuts

Ingredients

Donuts:

- 2 tsp red food coloring
- 1 egg, large
- 1 tsp vanilla extract
- 2 ½ tbsp melted butter
- ½ cup of buttermilk
- 1 tsp baking powder
- ½ tsp salt
- ½ cup of dark brown sugar
- 2 tbsp cocoa powder

- 1 cup of all-purpose flour

Cream cheese frosting:

- 1 to 2 tbsp milk
- 2 cups of confectioners' sugar
- 1 tsp vanilla extract
- 3 tablespoons unsalted butter, softened
- 3 oz. cream cheese softened

Directions

- Preheat your oven to 350°F.
- Coat a donut pan with cooking spray.
- Combine the dry ingredients in a big bowl.
- Mix up buttermilk, egg, vanilla, and melted butter in a separate bowl.
- Combine the wet ingredients with the flour mixture until just combined. Fold in the food coloring and mix till just combined.
- Scoop the mixture into the cups on the donut pan,

filling up to 2/3 full.

- Bake donuts in the oven until a toothpick inserted in the middle comes out clean, about 10 minutes.

- Remove from the oven and allow cooling for 5 minutes. Remove from the pan and set on a wire rack.

- Make the cream cheese frosting: Place cream cheese, vanilla extract, and butter in a big bowl and use an electric handheld mixer to beat the ingredients on medium-high speed until smooth.

- Turn the speed to low and add in confectioners' sugar and milk. Beat on high speed for about one to two minutes.

- Spread the frosting generously on warm donuts.

GLAZED PUMPKIN DONUTS

This baked cake donut recipe can be lightly glazed or covered in sugar-cinnamon mix.

Total Time: 25 minutes

Yield: 12 donuts

Ingredients

Donuts:

- 1/4 cup of softened butter
- 1/4 cup of milk
- 2 eggs
- 1 cup of pumpkin puree
- 1/4 tsp baking soda
- 1/2 tsp salt
- 1 1/2 tsp pumpkin pie spice
- 1 1/2 tsp baking powder
- 1/2 cup of packed brown sugar

- 2 cups of all-purpose flour

Glaze:

- 1 tsp vanilla extract
- 2 tbsp water
- 1/4 cup of melted butter
- 1 1/2 cups of confectioners' sugar

Directions

- Preheat your oven to 325°F.
- Coat a donut pan with the cooking spray. Line a baking sheet with parchment paper.
- In a big bowl, combine flour, baking soda, salt, pumpkin pie spice, baking powder, and brown sugar. Add in the softened butter, milk, eggs, and pumpkin puree.
- Mix the mixture with an electric hand mixer on a low speed until combined. Then, scoop the mixture into the donut pan.
- Place the batter in the oven and bake for 8 to 10 minutes or until donuts spring back when touched.

- In a small bowl, mix up confectioners' sugar, vanilla extract, water, and melted butter. Dip warm donuts into the mixture and place them on the baking sheet to cool. Enjoy!

Nutrition Information Per Serving

262 calories; sodium 303.5mg 12% DV; cholesterol 48mg 16% DV; fat 8.8g 14% DV; carbohydrates 42.8g 14% DV; protein 3.6g 7% DV.

VANILLA COCONUT DONUTS

These baked donuts are glazed with sugar and dusted with coconut flakes. Enjoy!

Total Time: 35 minutes

Yield: 6 donuts

Ingredients

Donuts:

- 1/2 cup of coconut flakes, unsweetened
- 1 tsp vanilla extract
- 1 cup of unsweetened applesauce
- 1/3 cup of coconut oil
- 1 cup of raw cane sugar, organic
- 1/2 cup of dairy-free vanilla coconut milk
- 1/4 tsp salt
- 1/2 tsp xanthan gum
- 1/4 tsp baking soda

- 1 1/2 tsp baking powder
- 1/4 cup of arrowroot powder
- 1/4 cup of potato starch
- 1/4 cup of garbanzo flour
- 3/4 cup of rice flour

Coconut Flake Coating:

- 1/2 cup of coconut flakes, unsweetened (plus extra if needed)
- 1 tbsp hot water (plus extra if needed)
- 1/2 cup of powdered sugar

Directions

- Preheat your oven to 350°F. Spray a 6-donut pan with cooking spray.
- In a bowl, combine rice flour, garbanzo flour, salt, xanthan gum, baking soda, baking powder, arrowroot, and potato starch. Set aside.
- Place coconut oil and milk into a medium pot and warm

over low heat till coconut oil melt (don't boil), stirring gently with a wooden spoon.

- Once the coconut oil is completely melted, turn off the heat and stir in sugar. When the sugar dissolves, add vanilla extract and applesauce and stir to blend the ingredients.

- Add the liquid mix to the dry ingredients and mix thoroughly until smooth. If needed, use an immersion blender to blend the batter until smooth.

- Add coconut flakes to the mixture and mix using a wooden spoon. Scoop the mixture into the prepared donut pan, filling halfway.

- Place the batter inside the preheated oven and bake for about 15 minutes at 350°F.

- Remove the donut pan from the oven and allow cooling for about 20 minutes.

- To remove the donut neatly, gently scrape the donut's sides and flip out the pan to get them out. You may use a toothpick to lift out the donuts from the pan.

- Make the glaze by combining one tablespoon of hot water at a time with the powdered sugar in a small bowl. Lightly coat the donuts with the glaze and place them inside a plate with the coconut flakes for coating.

Nutrition Information Per Serving

335 calories; sodium 217.2mg 9% DV; fat 17.3g 27% DV; carbohydrates 44.3g 14% DV; protein 2.4g 5% DV.

...OLATE DONUTS

...is is a fantastic recipe for chocolate donuts. If you desire, add some chocolate chips to the batter before baking. Enjoy!

Total Time: 40 minutes

Yield: 30 donuts

Ingredients

Donuts:

- 2 tbsp chocolate chips, optional
- 1 tbsp vegetable oil
- 2 tbsp melted butter
- 1 large egg, whisked
- 1 1/4 cups of 2% milk
- 1 tsp salt
- 2 tsp baking powder
- 1/4 cup of cocoa powder, unsweetened
- 1 1/2 cups of white sugar

- 2 cups of all-purpose flour

Glaze:

- 4 tbsp hot water (add more if needed)
- 6 cups of confectioners' sugar
- 6 tsp vanilla extract, divided

Directions

- Preheat your oven to 350°F.
- Spray a donut pan with cooking spray.
- In a big bowl, combine flour, salt, baking powder, cocoa, and sugar.
- In a separate bowl, mix up milk, 2 tsp vanilla extract, oil, butter, and egg. Add the wet ingredients to the flour mixture and mix until just combined (avoid overmixing). Stir in chocolate chips if using.
- Scoop the mixture into the greased donut pan and fill each cup to ¾ full.
- Place the donuts in the oven and bake for ten minutes or until the donuts spring back when pressed lightly.

- Remove the pan from the oven, allow cooling for about five minutes, then transfer the donuts to a sheet pan.

- To make the glaze, mix up the remaining vanilla extract, hot water, and confectioners' sugar.

- Put parchment paper under a wire rack. Set the donuts on the wire rack and coat with the glaze; allow the excess to drip on the parchment paper.

Nutrition Information Per Serving

189 calories; sodium 122.7mg 5% DV; cholesterol 9mg 3% DV; fat 1.8g 3% DV; carbohydrates 42.4g 14% DV; protein 1.6g 3% DV.

CREAMY GLAZED DONUTS

Total Time: 20 minutes

Yield: 10 donuts

Ingredients

Donuts:

- 1/2 teaspoon vanilla
- 1 1/2 tablespoons butter melted
- 1 large egg, beaten
- 1/2 cup of buttermilk
- 3/4 teaspoon salt
- 1 1/4 teaspoons baking powder
- 1 1/4 teaspoons cups of all-purpose flour
- 1/2 cup of granulated sugar

Glaze:

- 1/4 cup of milk
- 2 cups of powdered sugar

Directions

- Preheat your oven to 350°F.

- Coat donut pans with cooking spray.

- Combine flour, salt, baking powder, and sugar in a big bowl.

- Mix up buttermilk, vanilla, and egg in a separate bowl.

- Combine the wet ingredients with the flour mixture until just combined.

- Scoop the mixture into the cups on the donut pan, filling up to 2/3 full.

- Bake donuts in the oven until a toothpick inserted in the middle comes out clean, about 8 to 10 minutes.

- Remove from the oven and allow cooling for 5 minutes. Remove from the pan and set on a wire rack.

- Make the glaze by mixing the glaze ingredients in a bowl.

- Dip warm donuts into the glaze and set on the wire rack. If using, add sprinkles immediately after dipping into the glaze.

Nutrition Information Per Serving

185 calories; sodium 152mg 6% DV; cholesterol 19mg 6% DV; fat 3g 5% DV; carbohydrates 39g 13% DV; protein 3g 6% DV.

COCONUT LIME DONUTS

Total Time: 20 minutes

Yield: 6 donuts

Ingredients

Donuts:

- ½ cup of coconut milk
- 1 egg, large
- 2 ½ tbsp coconut oil, melted
- 2 tsp fresh lime zest
- ½ cup of granulated sugar
- ½ tsp salt
- 1 tsp baking powder
- 1 ¼ cups of all-purpose flour

Glaze:

- ⅛ tsp salt
- 1 tsp lime zest

- 1 ½ tbsp key lime juice
- 1 cup of confectioners' sugar

Optional decoration:

- 2 tsp lime zest
- ½ cup of shredded coconut, toasted

Directions

- Preheat your oven to 350°F.
- Coat a donut pan with cooking spray.
- Combine flour, salt, and baking powder in a big bowl.
- Mix up lime zest, sugar, egg, coconut milk, and melted coconut oil in a separate bowl.
- Combine the wet ingredients with the flour mixture until just combined.
- Scoop the mixture into the cups on the donut pan, filling up to 2/3 full.
- Bake donuts in the oven until a toothpick inserted in the middle comes out clean, about 10 to 12 minutes.

- Remove from the oven and allow cooling for 5 minutes. Remove from the pan and set on a wire rack.

- Make the glaze by combining the glaze ingredients in a bowl.

- Dip warm donuts into the glaze and place on the wire rack to set.

CREAM DONUTS WITH OREO

Total Time: 20 minutes

Yield: 6 donuts

Ingredients

Donuts:

- ½ cup of milk
- 2 ½ tbsp melted butter, unsalted
- 1 egg, large
- ½ tsp vanilla extract
- 1 tsp baking powder
- ¼ cup of cocoa powder
- ½ tsp salt
- ½ cup of light brown sugar
- 1 cup of all-purpose flour

Cream cheese frosting:

- 1 cup of crushed Oreo cookies

- 1 to 2 tbsp milk

- 1 ½ cups of confectioners' sugar

- ¼ tsp vanilla extract

- 2 tablespoons butter, softened

- 4 oz. cream cheese, softened

Directions

- Preheat your oven to 325°F.

- Coat a donut pan with baking spray.

- Combine the dry ingredients in a big bowl.

- Mix the wet ingredients until smooth in a separate bowl.

- Combine the wet ingredients with the dry ingredients until just combined.

- Scoop the mixture into the cups on the donut pan, filling up to 2/3 full.

- Bake donuts in the oven for about 10 to 12 minutes.

- Remove from the oven and allow cooling for 5 minutes.

Remove from the pan and set on a wire rack.

- Make the cream cheese frosting: Place cream cheese, vanilla extract, and butter in a big bowl and use an electric handheld mixer to beat the ingredients on medium-high speed until smooth.

- Turn the speed to low and add in confectioners' sugar and milk. Beat on high-speed for about one to two minutes.

- Spread the frosting generously on warm donuts and sprinkle with crushed Oreo cookies. Serve immediately.

LEMON POPPY SEED DONUTS

These wholesome donuts are fluffy, soft, delicious. Your donuts would be ready in just 20 minutes. Enjoy!

Total Time: 20 minutes

Yield: 6 donuts

Ingredients

Donuts:

- ½ cup of milk
- ½ tsp lemon extract
- 1 tsp vanilla extract
- 1 egg, large
- 2 ½ tbsp melted butter, unsalted
- 2 tsp grated lemon zest
- ½ cup of granulated sugar
- 2 ½ tbsp poppy seeds
- ½ tsp salt

- 1 ¼ tsp baking powder
- 1 ¼ cups of all-purpose flour

Glaze:

- 1 tsp grated lemon zest
- 1 tbsp lemon juice
- ¼ tsp salt
- 1 tbsp milk
- 1 ¼ cups of confectioners' sugar

Directions

- Preheat your oven to 325°F.
- Coat a donut pan with baking spray.
- Combine flour, poppy seeds, salt, and baking powder in a big bowl.
- Mix up lemon zest, sugar, egg, milk, melted butter, lemon extract, and vanilla extract until smooth in a separate bowl.
- Combine the wet ingredients with the flour mixture

until just combined.

- Scoop the mixture into the cups on the donut pan, filling up to 2/3 full.

- Bake donuts in the oven until a toothpick inserted in the middle comes out clean, about 10 to 12 minutes.

- Remove from the oven and allow cooling for 5 minutes. Remove from the pan and set on a wire rack.

- Make the glaze by combining the glaze ingredients in a bowl.

- Dip warm donuts into the glaze and place on the wire rack to set.

FLUFFY CAKE DONUTS

This is an easy and quick baked donut recipe that uses a powdered sugar glaze or chocolate icing. If you prefer, roll them in white sugar and cinnamon mix instead.

Total Time: 30 minutes

Yield: 12 donuts

Ingredients

Donuts:

- 1 tbsp shortening
- 1 tsp vanilla extract
- 2 large eggs, whisked
- 3/4 cup of milk
- 1 tsp salt
- 1/4 tsp ground cinnamon
- 1/4 tsp ground nutmeg
- 2 tsp baking powder

- 3/4 cup of white sugar
- 2 cups of all-purpose flour

Glaze:

- 1/2 tsp almond extract
- 2 tbsp hot water
- 1 cup of confectioners' sugar

Directions

- Preheat your oven to 325°F.
- Grease a donut pan lightly.
- Combine flour, salt, cinnamon, nutmeg, baking powder, and sugar in a big bowl.
- Add in shortening, vanilla, eggs, and milk. Mix until well combined.
- Scoop the mixture into the donut cups and fill up to ¾ full.
- Place donuts inside the preheated oven and bake until donuts spring back when touched, about 8 to 10

minutes.

- Allow slight cooling, and before you remove them from the oven.

- For the glaze, combine almond extract, hot water, and confectioners' sugar in a bowl. Dip your donuts in the glaze when you're serving.

- To make a chocolate glaze, stir half cup of chocolate chips into the glaze mixture.

Nutrition Information Per Serving

196 calories; sodium 272.3mg 11% DV; cholesterol 32.2mg 11% DV; fat 2.4g 4% DV; carbohydrates 39.9g 13% DV; protein 3.7g 7% DV.

LEMON BLUEBERRY DONUTS

These easy baked donuts are moist, fluffy, and delicious. You infuse with lemon and stuff them with fresh blueberries.

Total Time: 30 minutes

Yield: 10 to 12 donuts

Ingredients

Donuts:

- 1 cup of fresh blueberries
- 1 tbsp lemon zest, optional
- 1 tbsp lemon juice, fresh
- 1 tsp vanilla extract
- 2 tbsp vegetable oil
- ½ cup of buttermilk
- 1 egg, large
- ¼ tsp salt
- ½ tsp baking soda

- 1 tsp baking powder
- ½ cup of caster/granulated sugar
- 2 cups of all-purpose flour

Glaze:

- 2 to 4 tbsp milk
- 1 tsp pure vanilla extract
- 2 tsp lemon juice, fresh
- 2 cups of powdered sugar

Directions

- Preheat your oven to 350°F.
- Coat 2 donut pans with cooking spray.
- Combine flour, salt, baking soda, and baking powder in a bowl.
- Mix egg, zest, lemon juice, vanilla, oil, buttermilk, and sugar in a separate bowl until smooth.
- Combine the wet ingredients with the flour mixture. Mix until just combined. Fold the blueberries into the

mixture.

- Scoop the mixture into the cups on the donut pan, filling up to 2/3 full.

- Bake donuts in the oven until a toothpick inserted in the middle comes out clean, about 10 to 15 minutes.

- Remove from the oven and allow cooling for 5 minutes.

- Remove from the pan and set on a wire rack. Place a parchment paper beneath the wire rack.

- Make the glaze by combining milk, vanilla, lemon juice, and powdered sugar.

- Dip warm donuts into the glaze and place on the wire rack to set.

Nutrition Information Per Serving

280 calories; sodium 166mg; cholesterol 16mg; fat 3g; carbohydrates 61g; protein 3g; sugar 44g.

LEMON RASPBERRY DONUTS

These easy baked donuts are moist, fluffy, and delicious. You infuse with lemon, stuff them with fresh raspberries, and dunk in lemon glaze.

Total Time: 25 minutes

Yield: 12 donuts

Ingredients

Donuts:

- ¾ cup of fresh raspberries
- 1 lemon zest
- 1 tbsp lemon juice, fresh
- 2 tbsp vegetable oil
- ¼ cup of Greek yogurt
- ¼ cup of milk
- 1 tsp pure vanilla extract
- ½ cup of caster/granulated sugar

- 1 egg, large
- ¼ tsp salt
- ¼ tsp baking soda
- 2 tsp baking powder
- 2 cups of all-purpose flour

Glaze:

- 1 to 2 tbsp milk
- ½ tsp vanilla extract
- 1 tsp lemon juice, fresh
- 1 cup of powdered sugar

Directions

- Preheat your oven to 350°F.
- Coat 2 donut pans with cooking spray.
- Combine flour, salt, baking soda, and baking powder in a bowl.
- Mix egg, zest, lemon juice, oil, yogurt, milk, vanilla, and

sugar in a separate bowl until smooth.

- Combine the wet ingredients with the flour mixture. Mix until just combined. Fold the raspberries into the mixture and allow them to break up while mixing.

- Scoop the mixture into the cups on the donut pan, filling up to 2/3 full.

- Bake donuts in the oven until a toothpick inserted in the middle comes out clean, about 7 to 10 minutes.

- Remove from the oven and allow cooling for 5 minutes.

- Remove from the pan and set on a wire rack. Place a parchment paper beneath the wire rack.

- Make the glaze by combining milk, vanilla, lemon juice, and powdered sugar.

- Dip warm donuts into the glaze and place on the wire rack to set.

Nutrition Information Per Serving

190 calories; sodium 166mg; cholesterol 16mg; fat 3g; carbohydrates 37g; protein 3g; sugar 20g.

COOKIE AND CREAM DONUTS

This is an easy recipe for baked cookie and cream donuts. You will top the donuts with cream cheese glaze.

Total Time: 25 minutes

Yield: 18 donuts

Ingredients

Cookie and cream donut:

- ½ cup of crushed chocolate creme sandwich cookies
- 1 tsp vanilla extract
- 2 tbsp butter, melted & cooled
- 2 large eggs
- ⅔ cup of buttermilk
- A pinch of ground nutmeg
- A pinch of salt
- ½ tsp teaspoon baking soda
- 1 ½ tsp baking powder

- 2 tbsp cornstarch
- ⅔ cups of granulated sugar
- 1 ½ cups of all-purpose flour

Glaze:

- 2 tsp vanilla extract
- ½ cup of milk
- 4 cups of powdered sugar
- 4 oz. cream cheese, softened
- 1 cup of chocolate creme sandwich cookies, finely crushed

Directions

- Preheat your oven to 325°F.
- Coat 2 to 3 donut pans with baking spray.
- Combine flour, nutmeg, salt, baking soda, baking powder, cornstarch, and sugar.
- Mix up buttermilk, vanilla extract, melted butter, and eggs until smooth in a separate bowl.

- Add the wet ingredients to the flour mixture and mix until just combined. Gently mix the crushed cookies with the dough.

- Scoop the mixture into the cups on the donut pan, filling up to 2/3 full.

- Bake donuts in the oven for 10 to 12 minutes or until a toothpick inserted in the middle comes out clean.

- Remove from the oven and allow cooling for 5 minutes.

- Remove from the pan and set on a wire rack. Place a parchment paper beneath the wire rack.

- Make the cream cheese glaze by combining powdered sugar with cream cheese. Stir in vanilla extract and milk and mix until smooth.

- Pack half of the cream cheese glaze into a pastry bag with a tiny tip or plastic bag and cut off a small piece of the corner. Leave the remaining glaze in a bowl. Put the finely crushed cookies in a separate bowl.

- Dip each donut's top into the cream cheese glaze and let the excess drip off the donuts. Then, coat the donut in the finely crushed cookies.

- Set the donuts on the wire rack with the side of the cookie up. Drizzle the rest of the cream cheese glaze in the plastic or pastry bag over the donuts.

APPLE BUTTER DONUTS WITH WHOLE WHEAT

These delectable baked donuts are sweet and wholesome. Enjoy!

Total Time: 20 minutes

Yield: 12 donuts

Ingredients

Donuts:

- ⅛ tsp nutmeg
- ⅛ tsp cloves
- ½ tsp cinnamon
- ⅛ tsp baking soda
- ¾ tsp baking powder
- ½ tsp salt
- ¼ cup of packed brown sugar
- 1 cup of white whole wheat flour
- ½ tsp vanilla extract

- ¼ cup of melted unsalted butter
- ¼ cup of almond milk
- ½ cup of applesauce, unsweetened
- ⅔ cup of apple butter
- 1 large egg, beaten

Glaze:

- 1 tsp honey
- ¾ cup of powdered sugar
- ¼ cup of maple syrup
- A pinch of salt

Directions

- Preheat your oven to 350°F.
- Coat a donut pan with cooking spray.
- Combine flour, nutmeg, cloves, cinnamon, baking soda, baking powder, salt, and brown sugar in a bowl.
- Mix up egg, vanilla, melted butter, almond milk,

applesauce, and apple butter until smooth in a separate bowl.

- Combine the wet ingredients with the flour mixture and mix until just combined.

- Scoop the mixture into the donut pan and fill each cavity to ¾ full.

- Place the donut pan inside the preheated oven and bake for about eight to ten minutes.

- Remove the pan from the oven and allow cooling for two minutes before removing the donuts to a wire rack.

- For the glaze, add the glaze ingredients to a bowl and mix until smooth.

- Dip warm donuts into the glaze and return to the wire rack to set.

Nutrition Information Per Serving

168 calories; sodium 184mg; cholesterol 26mg; fat 5g; carbohydrates 31g; protein 2g; sugar 22g.

COFFEE DONUTS

These easy baked donuts are moist, fluffy, and delicious; you infuse coffee and top with coffee glaze. They are perfect for coffee lovers.

Total Time: 30 minutes

Yield: 8 donuts

Ingredients

Donuts:

- 1 tsp vanilla extract
- ¼ cup of vegetable oil
- ¼ cup of buttermilk
- ½ cup of caster/granulated sugar
- 1 egg, large
- ¼ tsp ground nutmeg
- ¼ tsp salt
- 1 tsp baking powder

- 1 ½ cups of all-purpose flour
- 2 tbsp instant coffee granules

Glaze:

- 2 ¼ cups of powdered sugar
- ½ tsp vanilla extract
- 1 tbsp instant coffee granules
- ¼ cup of warm milk

Directions

- Preheat your oven to 350°F.
- Coat a donut pan with cooking spray.
- Dissolve coffee granules in ¼ cup of hot water and set aside.
- Combine flour, nutmeg, salt, and baking powder in a bowl.
- Mix egg, coffee, vanilla, oil, buttermilk, and sugar in a separate bowl until smooth.
- Combine the wet ingredients with the flour mixture.

Mix until just combined. Fold the strawberries into the mixture.

- Scoop the mixture into the cups on the donut pan, filling up to 2/3 full.
- Bake donuts in the oven until a toothpick inserted in the middle comes out clean, about 8 to 10 minutes.
- Remove from the oven and allow cooling for 5 minutes.
- Remove from the pan and set on a wire rack. Place a parchment paper beneath the wire rack.
- Make the glaze; combine the warm milk, vanilla, and coffee until smooth in a bowl. Stir in powdered sugar and mix until smooth.
- Dip donuts into the glaze and place them on the wire rack to set.

Nutrition Information Per Serving

354 calories; sodium 156mg; cholesterol 24mg; fat 8g; carbohydrates 67g; protein 4g; sugar 48g.

CHAPTER 4: FILLED DONUTS

NUTELLA-FILLED DONUT MUFFINS

This amazing recipe will make you super delicious donut muffins.

Total Time: 55 minutes

Yield: 12 donut muffins

Ingredients

Donut Muffins:

- 1 (13 oz.) jar of chocolate-hazelnut spread (like Nutella)
- 1 tsp vanilla extract
- 1 egg
- 1/3 cup of vegetable oil
- 3/4 cup of milk
- 3/4 cup of white sugar

- 1/2 tsp ground cinnamon

- 1/2 tsp salt

- 1 1/2 tsp baking powder

- 1 3/4 cups of all-purpose flour

Cinnamon-Sugar Coating:

- 1 tsp ground cinnamon

- 1/3 cup of white sugar

- 3 tbsp butter, unsalted (or more if required)

Powdered Sugar Glaze:

- 2 tsp vanilla extract

- 1/4 cup of milk

- 1 1/2 cups sifted powdered sugar

Directions

- Preheat your oven to 350°F.

- Coat a 12-cup muffin tin with cooking oil.

- Mix up flour, cinnamon, salt, and baking powder in a

medium bowl.

- In a separate bowl, whisk together vanilla extract, egg, vegetable oil, milk, and ¾ cup of sugar.

- Add the wet ingredients to the flour mix and combine until blended.

- Scoop two tablespoons of the dough into each muffin tin. Place 1 to 2 teaspoons of Nutella in the middle of the donut muffins. Then, cover with 2 tablespoons of batter or until ¾ full.

- Place inside the preheated oven and bake for 18 to 22 minutes or until the bottoms and edges are browned. Avoid overbaking.

- Remove the donut muffins from the oven and allow sitting for five minutes. Then, shake out the donut muffins from the cup while they're still warm.

- Place the butter in a small heat-resistant bowl and melt in the microwave in ten-second intervals.

- Mix up cinnamon and sugar in a separate bowl. Dip the donut muffins into the melted butter and then into the cinnamon-sugar mix to coat.

- In a small bowl, combine vanilla extract, milk, and sugar. Dip the donuts into the glaze. Serve warm.

Nutrition Information Per Serving

454 calories; sodium 202.4mg 8% DV; cholesterol 24.8mg 8% DV; fat 18.8g 29% DV; carbohydrates 67.7g 22% DV; protein 5.1g 10% DV.

STRAWBERRY JAM FILLED DONUT CUPCAKES

These cupcakes are delectably moist and filled with jam. Top them with cinnamon-spiced buttercream icing. Enjoy!

Total Time: 1 hr. 5 min

Yield: 12 donut cupcakes

Ingredients

Donuts:

- 1/2 cup of butter, melted
- 1 tbsp honey
- 3 large eggs
- 1 cup of buttermilk
- 3 cups of all-purpose flour
- 2 tsp ground cinnamon
- 1/2 tsp ground cloves
- 1 tsp ground nutmeg
- 1 tsp baking soda

- 2 tsp baking powder
- 1 cup of white sugar

Coating:

- 1 tsp ground cinnamon
- ½ cup of granulated sugar

Cupcakes:

- ½ cup of seedless strawberry jam
- ½ cup of Greek yogurt
- ½ cup of melted unsalted butter
- 2 tsp vanilla extract
- ¾ cup of granulated sugar
- 2 eggs, large
- ¼ tsp salt
- ¼ tsp baking soda
- 1 tsp baking powder
- 1 ½ cups of cake flour

Frosting:

- ½ tsp ground cinnamon
- 2 to 3 tbsp milk
- 1 tsp vanilla extract
- 4 cups of powdered sugar
- 1 cup of unsalted butter, softened

Directions

For the donuts holes:

- Preheat your oven to 350°F.
- Grease a mini muffin pan lightly.
- Mix up the dry ingredients in a bowl.
- In a different bowl, combine butter, honey, eggs, and buttermilk. And then, stir into the flour mixture. Mix until well combined.
- Scoop one tablespoon of the batter into each tin in the muffin pan.
- Bake in the oven until a toothpick inserted in the

middle of the donut hole comes out clean, about ten minutes.

- Remove from the oven and allow to cool for about five minutes before transferring to a wire rack.

- Make the cinnamon-sugar mix by combining sugar and cinnamon in a bowl.

- Roll warm donut holes in the mix and coat them thoroughly. Set them on the wire rack.

For the cupcakes:

- Preheat your oven to 350°F and line a 12-cavity muffin pan with muffin cases.

- In a bowl, combine flour, salt, baking soda, and baking powder.

- In a separate bowl, mix eggs, yogurt, melted butter, vanilla extract, and sugar until smooth.

- Combine the wet ingredients with the flour mixture. Mix until well combined.

- Scoop the mixture into the prepared muffin cases, filling up to 2/3 full.

- Place in the oven and bake until a toothpick inserted at the middle comes out clean, about 15 to 20 minutes.

- Remove from the oven and allow cooling for five minutes in the pan before moving them to a wire rack to cool completely.

- Make the frosting; beat the butter until creamy and pale in a stand mixer or handheld mixer. Add 1/2 of the powdered sugar and mix until combined. Add the rest of the powdered sugar and mix until combined.

- Add in cinnamon, milk, and vanilla and mix until fluffy and light. If needed, add in more milk and mix again.

- Use a small knife or cupcake corer to scoop out the middle of the cupcakes. Fill the cooled cupcakes with strawberry jam.

- Pack the frosting into a piping bag and frost your cupcakes. Place a donut hole on each cupcake and drizzle with runny jam.

Nutrition Information Per Serving

766 calories; sodium 223mg; cholesterol 117mg; fat 29g; carbohydrates 124g; protein 6g; sugar 100g

PEANUT BUTTER JELLY DONUTS

The amazing donuts are so light, fluffy, and delicious. You fill the donuts with raspberry jam and top with creamy peanut butter glaze.

Total Time: 50 minutes

Yield: 8 donuts

Ingredients

Donuts:

- 1 ½ tsp pure vanilla extract
- 2 tbsp melted butter, unsalted
- ¼ cup of yogurt
- ¼ cup of milk
- ⅓ cup of packed light brown sugar
- 1 large egg
- ¼ tsp ground nutmeg
- ½ tsp ground cinnamon

- ½ tsp salt
- ¼ tsp baking soda
- 1 tsp baking powder
- 1 cup of all-purpose flour

Filling:

- ¾ cup of raspberry jam

Peanut Butter Glaze:

- 2 tbsp whipping cream
- ¾ cup of powdered sugar
- 2 tbsp peanut butter
- Salt to taste

Directions

- Preheat your oven to 325°F.
- Coat a donut pan with baking spray and set aside.
- In a big bowl, mix up flour, nutmeg, cinnamon, salt, baking soda, and baking powder.

- In a separate bowl, whisk together yogurt, milk, brown sugar, and egg until smooth. Stir in vanilla and melted butter and keep whisking until well combined.

- Pour the dry ingredients into the flour mixture and mix until blended. Avoid over mixing.

- Scoop the donut into the cavities of the donut pan, filling up to ⅔ full.

- Bake until a toothpick inserted at the middle of the donut comes out clean, about 9 to 10 minutes.

- Allow cooling for about 2 minutes, then place on a wire rack. Let donut cool enough for handling.

- Fill a squeezy bottle or pastry bag with raspberry jam. Poke a hole on the side of the donuts and gently inject jam into each donut. Flip the donut around and squeeze some jam in on the other side too.

- Once you have injected all the donuts with jam, make your peanut butter glaze. Mix cream, salt, powdered sugar, and peanut butter in a bowl until creamy.

- Dip the donuts into the glaze and place on the wire rack

to set. Enjoy!

JELLY DONUT CUPCAKES

This is a delicious recipe that friends and family will enjoy. A baked vanilla-flavored cake that is filled with strawberry jam and dusted with powdered sugar.

Total Time: 1 hr. 20 min

Yield: 24 donut cupcakes

Ingredients

- 2 tbsp confectioners' sugar (for dusting)
- 1 (12 oz.) jar of seedless raspberry jam
- 4 eggs
- 1 cup of vegetable oil
- 1 cup of whole milk
- 1 (3.5 oz.) package instant French vanilla pudding mix
- 1 (18.5 oz.) package yellow cake mix

Directions

- Preheat your oven to 350°F.

- Coat 24 muffin tins with cooking spray. Line each cup with a paper liner.

- In a big bowl, combine eggs, vegetable oil, milk, instant French vanilla pudding mix, and yellow cake mix. Use an electric hand mixer to blend the ingredients until moistened and smooth.

- Scoop the mixture into the muffin cups, filling halfway.

- Bake in the oven for 15 to 18 min. or until lightly golden brown.

- Remove from the oven and allow cooling. Make a hole of about 1 ½ inch long and ¾ inch width in the center of each cupcake.

- Fill the holes with raspberry jam and sprinkle confectioners' sugar lightly on the cupcakes.

Nutrition Information Per Serving

246 calories; sodium 216.4mg 9% DV; cholesterol 32.5mg 11% DV; fat 12.9g 20% DV; carbohydrates 31g 10% DV; protein 2.3g 5% DV.

CHEESECAKE STUFFED DONUTS

This is an easy recipe for fluffy donuts stuffed with cream cheese, coated with cinnamon sugar, and top with raspberry jam. Enjoy!

Total Time: 40 minutes

Yield: 6 donuts

Ingredients

Donuts:

- ¼ cup of heavy cream
- 4 tbsp unsalted butter, room temperature
- ¼ tsp fine salt
- 2 ½ cups of all-purpose flour
- ⅓ of cup granulated sugar
- 4 egg yolks
- 2 ¼ tsp instant yeast
- ½ tspter vanilla extract

- 1 tsp minced lemon zest
- ½ cup of warm water

Filling:

- 1 tsp pure vanilla extract
- ¼ cup of powdered sugar
- ¼ cup of heavy cream
- 8 oz. cream cheese, room temperature

Toppings:

- 2 tbsp melted unsalted butter
- 2 tsp ground cinnamon
- ¾ cup of granulated sugar
- Raspberry jam

Directions

- Combine sugar, eggs, yeast, vanilla, zest, and water in a stand mixer bowl, fitted with the dough attachment.
- Slowly add in flour and salt and mix until combined.

Add butter to the mixture and mix on a medium speed until it forms a smooth, sticky dough.

- Place the dough on a greased bowl and cover with a lid. Allow the dough to rise to double, about 1 hour to 1½ hours.

- In the meantime, prepare the cheesecake filling. Combine cream cheese, vanilla, sugar, and cream in a bowl. Mix with an electric mixer until smooth and fluffy. Set aside.

- Remove the dough from the bowl and place it on a lightly floured surface. Roll out the dough to half-inch thick and use a round cookie cutter to cut out six dough rounds.

- Set the rounds on a lined baking sheet, ensuring there's space between them. Cover the dough and allow to rise for 30 minutes or until puffy.

- Preheat your oven to 375°F and bake the donuts until golden brown, about ten minutes. Remove from the oven and allow cooling.

- Once cooled enough to be handled, fill a piping bag

fitted with a pointed tip with cream cheese. Poke a hole on the side of each donut and inject the donuts with cream cheese.

- Combine sugar and cinnamon in a bowl. Dip warm donuts into the melted butter and then coat with the sugar-cinnamon mix.

- Top each donut with a dollop of cream cheese and drizzle jam over the donuts. Serve warm.

STRAWBERRY DONUTS

These easy baked donuts are moist, fluffy, and delicious. You stuff them with fresh strawberries and top them with strawberry glaze.

Total Time: 30 minutes

Yield: 10 donuts

Ingredients

Donuts:

- ½ cup of fresh strawberries, diced
- 2 tsp vanilla extract
- ¼ cup of vegetable oil
- ½ cup of buttermilk
- ½ cup caster/granulated sugar
- 1 egg, large
- ¼ tsp salt
- 1 tsp baking powder

- 1 ½ cups of all-purpose flour

Glaze:

- 1 to 2 tbsp milk
- 2 cups of powdered sugar
- 1 tsp vanilla extract
- 2 large fresh strawberries. diced

Directions

- Preheat your oven to 350°F.
- Coat 2 to 3 donut pans with cooking spray.
- Combine flour, salt, and baking powder in a bowl.
- Mix egg, vanilla, oil, buttermilk, and sugar in a separate bowl until smooth.
- Combine the wet ingredients with the flour mixture. Mix until just combined. Fold the strawberries into the mixture.
- Scoop the mixture into the cups on the donut pan, filling up to 2/3 full.

- Bake donuts in the oven until a toothpick inserted in the middle comes out clean, about 10 to 12 minutes.

- Remove from the oven and allow cooling for 5 minutes.

- Remove from the pan and set on a wire rack. Place a parchment paper beneath the wire rack.

- Make the glaze; puree the chopped strawberries until smooth. Then, mix the puree with powdered sugar and vanilla.

- Add one or two tablespoons of milk to the glaze and mix until your desired thickness is reached.

- Dip donuts into the glaze and place them on the wire rack to set.

Nutrition Information Per Serving

272 calories; sodium 24mg; cholesterol 19mg; fat 6g; carbohydrates 50g; protein 3g; sugar 36g.

CHERRIES & CREAM FILLED DONUTS

Total Time: 2 hrs. 15 min.

Yield: 18 donuts

Ingredients

Donuts:

- 1 egg, whisked lightly
- 2 tbsp melted unsalted butter
- ½ tsp kosher salt
- ¼ cup of granulated sugar
- 2½ cups of all-purpose flour
- 1 cup of warm water
- 1 (¼ oz.) package instant yeast

Baking:

- ½ cup of melted butter

Coating:

- 1 cup of granulated sugar

Filling:

- 1 (15 oz.) can Oregon Fruit Cherries
- 1/2 cup powdered sugar
- 2 cups heavy whipping cream, cold

Directions

- Add warm water and yeast into the bowl of a stand mixer fitted with the dough attachment.
- Add in flour, egg, melted butter, salt, and sugar. Mix on a low speed to combine. Change to medium speed and mix until thoroughly combined and a sticky dough is formed.
- Transfer the dough to a greased bowl and cover firmly. Allow the dough to rise to double for about one hour.
- Remove the dough from the bowl and place it on a lightly floured surface. Roll out the dough to ¼-inch thick and use a round cookie cutter to cut out 18 rounds of dough. Pack the scraps and repress with your hands.
- Set the rounds on a lined baking sheet, ensuring there's space between them. Cover the dough with a clean

towel and allow to rise for 30 minutes or until puffy.

- Preheat your oven to 375°F. Brush donuts with melted butter and bake the donuts until golden brown, about ten minutes. Ensure you rotate the baking sheet halfway through to ensure even baking.

- Remove from the oven and allow slight cooling. Brush the donuts with butter.

- Turn your oven broiler to high and place 1 tray of donuts at a time under the broiler until the butter begins to bubble or for one to two minutes. Repeat the process for the rest of the donuts until all donuts are broiled.

- Once the donuts are cooled enough to be handled, coat them with granulated sugar.

- Make the filling; ensure you chill the stand mixer bowl ahead of time. Then, place the cold whipping cream inside the chilled bowl of the stand mixer fitted with a whisk attachment.

- Whisk at high speed until soft peaks form, scraping the bowl frequently. Add in three tablespoons of cherry juice and powdered sugar and continue whipping until thoroughly combined.

- Drain the cherries and chop them into small pieces. Gently mix the chopped cherries with the cream and then pack the filling into a plastic bag fitted with a pointed tip.

- Poke a hole on the side of each donut using a skewer and inject the cherry cream filling into the donuts.

- Serve the donuts immediately.

APPLE PIE DONUTS

This delicious donut recipe uses apple pie filling and cinnamon sugar coating.

Total Time: 40 minutes

Yield: 14 donuts

Ingredients

Donuts:

- 1 teaspoon apple pie spice
- 1 teaspoon vanilla
- 3 tablespoon butter melted, salted
- 3/4 cup of buttermilk
- 2 large eggs
- 3/4 cup of brown sugar
- 1/2 teaspoon baking soda
- 1 1/2 teaspoons baking powder
- 1 1/2 cups of flour

Apple Pie Filling:

- 1 tablespoon flour

- 1 teaspoon apple pie spice

- 3 tablespoons brown sugar

- 1 1/2 tablespoons salted butter

- 1 1/4 cups of diced gala apples (about 2 apples)

Coating:

- 1 tablespoon salted butter, melted

- 1 tablespoon cinnamon

- 1/4 cup of white granulated sugar

Directions

- Start by making the apple pie filling. Peel your apples; core and dice them.

- Place a saucepan over medium heat. Add in butter and brown sugar - stir until butter melts.

- Add the apple pie spice and diced apples. Stir, cover the pan, and cook until the apples become soft.

- Uncover the pan and add in flour to thicken the mixture. Stir and cook for about one minute. Remove from heat and set aside.

- Preheat your oven to 350°F. Coat a donut pan with cooking spray.

- In a bowl, combine flour, baking powder, baking soda, and apple pie spice.

- In a separate bowl, whisk eggs, vanilla, melted butter, buttermilk, and sugar together. Add the wet ingredients to the flour mixture and mix until combined.

- Add the apple pie filling and mix thoroughly with a spatula. Scoop the mixture into the cups on the donut pan, filling up to 2/3 full.

- Bake donuts in the oven for 10 to 12 minutes or until a toothpick inserted in the middle comes out clean.

- Remove from the oven and allow cooling for 5 minutes. Remove from the pan and set on a wire rack.

- Combine sugar and cinnamon in a bowl. Dip warm donuts into the melted butter and coat with the cinnamon-sugar mix. Place on the wire rack to set.

Nutrition Information Per Serving

200 calories; sodium 118mg; cholesterol 37mg; fat 6g; carbohydrates 35g; protein 3g; sugar 22g.

APRICOT PLUM DONUTS

Total Time: 3 hrs. 30 min.

Yield:

Ingredients

Donuts:

- 5 cups of all-purpose flour

- 1/4 cup of sugar

- 2 large eggs, whisked

- 1/3 cup of warm water

- 4 1/2 teaspoons active dry yeast

- 1/3 cup of vegan butter

- 1 1/2 cups of non-dairy milk

Filling:

- A dash of ground clove

- A dash of ground cinnamon

- 1/2 cup of maple syrup

- 3 tablespoons plum preserve
- 5 apricots, diced

Coating:

- 2 teaspoon ground cinnamon
- 1 cup of sugar

Directions

- Place milk in a pan and warm over medium heat. Add butter and heat until melted. Remove from heat and allow to cool slightly.
- In a bowl, mix yeast with warm water and allow to dissolve for five minutes. There will be a layer of foam on top when it's ready.
- Pour the yeast mixture into a stand mixer fitted with the dough attachment. Add in milk, sugar, eggs, and 1/2 of the flour.
- Mix on a low speed until combined. Then, change to medium speed and mix until thoroughly mixed and a sticky dough is formed.

- Transfer the dough to a greased bowl and cover firmly. Allow the dough to rise to double for about one hour.

- Punch down the dough, cover it tightly, and allow it to rise for one more hour.

- Meanwhile, make your apricot plum filling by combining apricots, clove, cinnamon, maple syrup, and plum preserve in a small pan. Simmer until apricots are tender, about 15 to 20 minutes. Allow cooling.

- Once filling is cold and the dough is ready, preheat your oven to 375°F.

- Remove the dough from the bowl and place it on a lightly floured surface. Roll out the dough to half-inch thick and use a round cookie cutter to cut out rounds.

- Put a round of dough on a cookie sheet lined with parchment paper. Spoon apricot-plum mixture in the middle of the dough round and brush the edge with water or milk. Put another dough round over the filling and press the edge tightly to seal. Be careful not to press out the filling.

- Repeat the above process for the remaining dough

rounds. Cover the donuts and allow rising for about 30 minutes.

- Bake in the oven until the bottoms become brown, about 12 to 15 minutes.

- Remove from the oven and allow slight cooling. Dip warm donuts into the melted vegan butter and coat with sugar-cinnamon mix.

CHAPTER 5: DONUT HOLES

CHOCOLATE CAKE DONUT HOLES

These homemade treats are fun to make. You can use a mini muffin pan for baking them and then topping with vanilla glaze and your favorite sprinkles.

Total Time: 35 minutes

Yield: 24 donut holes (12 servings)

Ingredients

Donuts:

- 1 tsp vanilla extract
- 2 tbsp of brewed coffee, slightly cooled
- 4 tbsp dairy-free butter or unsalted butter, melted and slightly cooled
- 1 egg, lightly whisked
- 1/2 cup of packed light brown sugar

- 1/2 cup of milk
- 1/4 tsp salt
- 1/4 tsp baking soda
- 1/4 cup of cocoa powder, unsweetened
- 1 1/4 of cups all-purpose flour

Glaze:

- 4 to 5 tbsp milk
- pinch of salt
- 2 tsp vanilla extract
- 2 cups of confectioners' sugar
- sprinkles, for garnish (optional)

Directions

- Preheat your oven to 325°F.
- Coat a mini muffin pan with a cooking spray.
- Combine flour, salt, baking soda, and cocoa powder in a big bowl.

- Mix up milk, vanilla, coffee, butter, egg, and sugar in a separate bowl.

- Combine the wet ingredients with the flour mixture and mix until blended.

- Scoop 1 tablespoon of the batter into each cavity of the muffin pan.

- Bake in the oven until a toothpick inserted at the center comes out clean, for 10 to 12 minutes.

- Remove the donut holes from the oven and allow cooling for three to five minutes in the pan. Move the donut holes to a wire rack and let them cool for another ten minutes.

- In the meantime, make your glaze. In a small bowl, combine confectioners' sugar, salt, and vanilla. Slowly stir in the milk, adding one tablespoon at a time until your preferred consistency.

- Place a parchment paper beneath the wire rack to prevent the glaze from dripping on your counter.

- Roll the donut holes in the glaze and coat with the

sprinkle if you're using. Place them on a wire rack to set.

Nutrition Information Per Serving (serving size: 2 donut holes)

205 calories; sodium 114mg; cholesterol 27mg; fat 5g; carbohydrates 38g; protein 3g.

CINNAMON DONUT HOLES

Total Time: 35 minutes

Yield: 40 donut holes

Ingredients

Donuts:

- 1 cup of milk
- 2 ⅔ cups of all-purpose flour
- 1 tsp vanilla extract
- 1 tsp nutmeg
- ¾ tsp salt
- ¼ tsp baking soda
- 1 ½ tsp baking powder
- 2 large eggs, beaten
- ⅓ cup of packed brown sugar
- ½ cup of granulated sugar
- ¼ cup of vegetable oil

- 4 tbsp softened butter

Coating:

- 3 tbsp cinnamon-sugar mixture

Directions

- Preheat your oven to 325°F.
- Spray a donut hole pan or mini muffin pan with cooking spray.
- In a big bowl, combine flour, nutmeg, salt, baking soda, and baking powder.
- In a separate bowl, mix up eggs, milk, butter, vanilla, sugars, and vegetable oil until smooth.
- Add the wet ingredients to the flour mixture and mix well until combined.
- Scoop 1 tablespoon of the batter into each cavity of the donut hole or mini muffin pan.
- Bake in the oven until pale golden brown and a toothpick inserted at the center of the donut holes comes out clean, about 15 to 17 minutes.

- Remove from the oven and allow slight cooling.

- Loosen the edges of the donut hole and gently transfer them to a wire rack to cool. Grease the pan again and bake the remaining batch.

- Coat warm donut holes with the cinnamon-sugar mix.

Nutrition Information Per Serving (serving size: 1 donut hole)

80 calories; sodium 75mg; cholesterol 15mg; fat 3g; carbohydrates 12g; protein 1g; sugars 6g.

DONUT HOLES WITH VANILLA CREAM GLAZE

Total Time: 20 minutes

Yield: 24 donut holes

Ingredients

Donut holes:

- 1 tsp vanilla
- 1 egg, large
- ¼ cup of neutral oil
- ½ cup of sugar
- ½ cup of buttermilk
- A pinch salt
- ½ tbsp baking powder
- 3 tbsp cornstarch
- 1 ¼ cups of all-purpose flour

Coating:

- ⅓ cup of unsalted butter, melted

- 1 tablespoon ground cinnamon
- ⅔ cup of sugar

Vanilla Cream Cheese Icing:

- 2 tbsp milk
- 1 tsp vanilla extract
- ½ cup of confectioner's sugar
- 2 oz. softened cream cheese, room temperature

Directions

- Preheat your oven to 400°F.
- Coat a 24-cavity mini muffin pan.
- In a bowl, combine flour, salt, baking powder, and cornstarch.
- In a separate bowl, whisk together milk, vanilla extract, confectioners' sugar, and cream cheese until smooth.
- Combine the wet ingredients with the dry ingredients and mix until just combined.
- Scoop one tablespoon of the batter into each cavity of

the muffin pan.

- Bake in the oven until a toothpick inserted in the middle of the donut hole comes out clean, about 9 to 12 minutes.

- Allow cooling in the pan for five minutes. Remove from the pan and set on a wire rack to sit for five minutes.

- Combine sugar and cinnamon in a bowl. Dip the donut holes inside the melted butter and then coat with the sugar-cinnamon mix.

- To make the cream cheese icing, combine all the ingredients in a bowl and mix until smooth.

- Drizzle the icing lightly over the donut holes. Enjoy!

Note: If you prefer, spice the cinnamon sugar mix with some ground cardamom, nutmeg, ginger, cloves.

Nutrition Information Per Serving (2 donut holes)

133 calories; sodium 39mg 2% DV; cholesterol 16mg 5% DV; fat 6g 9% DV; carbohydrates 18g 6% DV; protein 1g 2% DV; sugar 12g 13% DV.

RED VELVET DONUT HOLES

Total Time: 30 minutes

Yield: 24 donut holes (12 servings)

Ingredients

Donut Holes:

- 1 tsp distilled white vinegar
- 1 tsp red food coloring
- 1 tsp vanilla extract
- 1 egg
- 2 tbsp melted butter
- ⅔ cup of granulated sugar
- ½ cup of buttermilk
- ¼ tsp salt
- ½ tsp baking soda
- 3 tbsp cocoa powder, unsweetened
- 1 cup of all-purpose flour

Glaze:

- 2 tbsp milk, or more as needed
- ½ tsp vanilla extract
- 1 ½ cups of powdered sugar
- 2 oz. cream cheese softened to room temperature

Directions

- Preheat your oven to 375°F.
- Coat a 24-count mini muffin pan with cooking spray.
- Combine flour, salt, baking soda, and cocoa powder in a big bowl.
- Mix up buttermilk, vinegar, red food coloring, vanilla, egg, melted butter, and sugar in a separate bowl.
- Add the wet ingredient to the flour mixture and mix until blended.
- Scoop one tablespoon of the mixture into the cavities of the mini muffin pan.
- Bake the donut holes in the oven until a toothpick

inserted into the donut hole comes out clean, about 10 to 12 minutes.

- Remove from the oven and allow cooling in the pan for five to ten minutes. Then, transfer to a wire rack.

- Make the glaze by combining cream cheese, milk, vanilla, and powdered sugar in a bowl. Mix well until smooth.

- Dip the donut holes in the glaze and place them on the wire rack for the glaze to set.

NUTELLA FILLED DONUT HOLES

When you bite into these delicious treats, Nutella oozes out.

Total Time: 40 minutes

Yield: 24 servings

Ingredients

Donut:

- 1/2 cup of whole milk
- 3/4 cup of all-purpose flour
- 1 teaspoon vanilla extract
- 1/4 teaspoon salt
- 1/4 teaspoon ground cinnamon
- 1/4 teaspoon baking soda
- 3 teaspoons baking powder
- 1 large egg
- 3 tablespoons light brown sugar
- 4 tablespoons golden caster sugar

- 1/4 cup of vegetable oil

Filling:

- 100g Nutella

Sugarcoating:

- 1/2 teaspoon cinnamon
- 1/2 cup of granulated sugar
- 1/4 cup of unsalted butter, melted

Directions

- Preheat your oven to 325°F.
- Coat a 24-cup mini muffin pan.
- In a bowl, combine flour, salt, cinnamon, baking soda, and baking powder.
- In a separate bowl, mix up egg, milk, oil, vanilla, and sugars. Add the wet ingredients to the flour mixture and mix until just combined.
- Scoop 1 tablespoon of the batter into each cavity of the muffin pan.

- Bake in the oven for ten minutes or until a toothpick inserted at the center comes out clean.

- In the meantime, make the sugar coating by combining cinnamon and sugar in a bowl. Place the melted butter in a separate bowl.

- Remove the donut holes from the oven and allow cooling. Once cooled enough to be handled, dip them in the melted butter and coat with the cinnamon-sugar mix.

- Make a hole inside the donut holes and pipe a little Nutella into each donut hole with a small star nozzle.

MOIST CHOCOLATE DONUT HOLES

Enjoy these moist chocolate donut holes coated with a sweet glaze.

Total Time: 45 minutes

Yield: 36 donut holes

Ingredients

Donut holes:

- 3 tbsp melted butter
- 2 tsp pure vanilla extract
- 1/4 cup of Greek yogurt (you can use your favorite)
- ¾ cup of milk, room temperature
- 2 large eggs, whisked
- ¼ tsp salt
- 1 tsp baking soda
- 1 tsp baking powder
- ½ cup of cocoa powder, unsweetened

- 1 cup of granulated sugar
- 2 cups of all-purpose flour

Glaze:

- 1 tsp lemon juice
- 1 tsp pure vanilla extract
- ¼ cup of heavy cream
- 1 ¾ of cups confectioners' sugar

Directions

- Preheat your oven to 375°F.
- Coat a 24-cup mini muffin pan with cooking spray.
- In a big bowl, sift and combine flour, cocoa powder, and sugar. Add salt, baking soda, and baking powder and stir to incorporate the ingredients.
- Mix up eggs, vanilla, yogurt, and milk until smooth in a different bowl. Stir in melted butter.
- Combine the wet ingredients with the flour mixture. Mix until just combined. Avoid overmixing.

- Scoop one tablespoon of the batter into each tin of the muffin pan.

- Bake in the oven until a toothpick inserted in the middle of the donut hole comes out clean, about ten minutes.

- Allow cooling in the pan for five minutes. Remove from the pan and set on a wire rack to sit for five minutes before coating with glaze.

- To make the glaze, combine confectioners' sugar, lemon juice, vanilla, and milk until smooth in a bowl.

- Place a baking sheet beneath the wire rack. Dip warm donut holes into the glaze and place on the wire rack to set.

- If you prefer, you may repeat dipping the donut hole into the glaze two to three times for a thicker coating.

CREAM CHEESE DONUT HOLES

Total Time: 20 minutes

Yield: 15 donut holes

Ingredients

Donut holes:

- ½ to 1 tsp red food coloring
- ¾ tsp distilled white vinegar
- 1 tsp pure vanilla extract
- ½ tbsp olive oil
- 2 tbsp Greek yogurt
- 2 tbsp melted unsalted butter, cooled
- ⅓ cup plus 1 tbsp buttermilk
- 1 egg, whisked lightly
- ¼ tsp Kosher salt
- ½ tsp baking soda
- ½ tsp baking powder

- ¼ cup of lightly packed brown sugar
- ¼ cup of white granulated sugar
- 3 tbsp cocoa powder
- 1 cup of cake flour

Cream Cheese Topping:

- ½ tsp vanilla extract
- 2 tbsp heavy cream
- ½ cup of powdered sugar
- ¼ cup of cream cheese, softened

Directions

- Preheat the oven to 375°F.
- Coat a mini muffin pan with cooking spray.
- Mix up flour, salt, baking powder, baking soda, brown sugar, sugar, and cocoa powder in a bowl.
- In a separate bowl, mix up buttermilk, vinegar, yogurt, and egg. You may use a hand mixer. Stir in cooled melted butter and mix well.

- Combine the wet ingredients with the flour mixture. Mix until just combined. Stir in red food coloring as needed.

- Scoop 1 tablespoon of the batter into each cup of the muffin pan.

- Bake in the oven until a toothpick inserted into the donut comes out clean, about 9 to 12 minutes. Remove from the oven and allow cooling in the pan for ten minutes. Transfer to a wire rack or baking sheet to cool.

- Make the cream cheese by combining the glaze ingredients in a bowl. Allow sitting for about ten minutes.

- Then, drizzle the glaze over the donut holes and enjoy it!

APPLE CIDER DONUT HOLES

These donut holes are super moist and are flavored with apple cider. This recipe is perfect for a cozy fall morning. You can also make donuts with this recipe.

Total Time: 45 minutes

Yield: 32 donut holes or 14 donuts

Ingredients

Donut holes:

- 1 tsp pure vanilla extract
- ½ cup of buttermilk, room temperature
- ½ cup of granulated sugar
- ½ cup of packed dark or dark brown sugar
- 2 tbsp melted unsalted butter, melted
- 1 egg, large
- ¼ tsp salt
- ¼ tsp ground cloves

- 1 tsp ground cinnamon
- 1 tsp baking soda
- ¾ tsp baking powder
- 2 cups of all-purpose flour
- 1 ¼ cups apple cider

Topping:

- ¼ cup of unsalted butter, melted
- 1 tsp ground cinnamon
- ¾ cup of granulated sugar

Directions

- Pour apple cider vinegar into a small pan and cook over low-medium heat for 15 to 20 minutes. If you desire, add orange slices, spices, and cinnamon stick to the vinegar for flavor.
- Once the vinegar is reduced, allow cooling in the fridge as you get the other ingredients ready.
- Preheat your oven to 350°F. Coat a donut pan or mini

muffin pan with cooking spray.

- In a big bowl, combine flour, salt, cloves, cinnamon, baking soda, and baking powder.

- In a separate bowl, mix granulated sugar, brown sugar, melted butter, and egg until smooth. Stir in half cup of refrigerated apple cider vinegar, vanilla, and buttermilk.

- Combine the wet ingredients with the flour mixture and mix until just combined.

- To make donut holes, scoop one tablespoon of the mixture into the mini muffin pan's tins.

- To make donuts, scoop the batter into a big plastic bag and cut off 1 corner. Squeeze the mixture into the greased donut pan and fill each cup to 2/3 full.

- Bake for until a toothpick inserted comes out clean, about 9 to 10 minutes.

- To make the glaze, combine cinnamon and sugar in a bowl. Dip your warm donut or donut holes in the melted butter and then coat with sugar-cinnamon mix.

PUMPKIN DONUT HOLES

This easy donut hole recipe is perfect as a fall treat. Enjoy!

Total Time: 30 minutes

Yield: 24 donut holes

Ingredients

Donut holes:

- 1/2 cup of milk
- 3/4 cup of canned plain pumpkin (this is not pumpkin pie filling)
- 1 tsp pure vanilla extract
- 1 egg, large
- 1/2 cup of light brown sugar
- 1/3 cup of canola oil
- 1/8 tsp ground cloves
- 1/2 tsp allspice
- 1/2 tsp nutmeg

- 1/2 tsp cinnamon
- 1/2 tsp salt
- 2 tsp baking powder
- 1 3/4 cups of all-purpose flour

For the Coating:

- 2 tbsp cinnamon
- ⅔ cup of granulated sugar
- 4 tbsp melted unsalted butter

Directions

- Preheat your oven to 375°F.
- Coat a 24-cavity mini muffin with cooking spray.
- Combine flour, cloves, allspice, nutmeg, cinnamon, salt, and baking powder in a bowl.
- Mix up milk, pumpkin, vanilla, egg, brown sugar, and oil in a separate bowl. Mix until smooth.
- Combine the wet ingredients with the flour mixture and mix until just combined. Avoid overmixing.

- Scoop one tablespoon of the batter into each cavity of the muffin pan.

- Bake in the oven until a toothpick inserted in the middle of the donut hole comes out clean, about 10 to 12 minutes.

- Allow cooling in the pan for five minutes. Remove from the pan and set on a wire rack to sit for five minutes.

- Combine sugar and cinnamon in a bowl. Dip the donut holes inside the melted butter and then coat with the sugar-cinnamon mix.

APPLE CINNAMON DONUT HOLES

This donut hole recipe will make you super soft donut holes with crusty sugar-cinnamon coating you can enjoy as a breakfast treat.

Total Time: 22 minutes

Yield: 36 donut holes (18 servings)

Ingredients

Donut holes:

- 1 tsp vanilla
- ½ cup of milk
- 1 cup of applesauce, unsweetened
- 1 egg
- ½ cup of brown sugar
- ¼ cup of unsalted butter, melted
- ½ tsp salt
- 1 tsp cinnamon

- 2 tsp baking powder
- 1 ¾ cups of all-purpose flour

Sugar-Cinnamon Coating:

- 1 tsp cinnamon
- ½ cup of granulated sugar
- ¼ cup of melted unsalted butter

Directions

- Preheat your oven to 350°F.
- Coat a mini muffin tin with cooking spray.
- In a big bowl, mix up flour, salt, cinnamon, and baking powder.
- Mix brown sugar and butter until smooth in a separate bowl; you may use a hand mixer for a quick result. Add in the egg and mix again. Stir in vanilla, milk, and applesauce.
- Add the wet ingredients to the flour mixture and mix until just combined.

- Scoop one tablespoon of the batter into each tin of the mini muffin pan.

- Bake in the oven until done, for 12 to 13 minutes. Remove from the oven and allow cooling in the pan for ten minutes. Transfer to a wire rack or baking sheet to cool.

- Combine cinnamon and sugar. Then, dip the donut holes in the butter and then coat with the cinnamon-sugar mixture. Place on the wire rack or baking sheet to set.

Nutrition Information Per Serving (2 donut holes)

140 calories; sodium 123mg; cholesterol 24mg; fat 6g; carbohydrates 21g; protein 2g; fiber 2g.

OTHER BOOKS BY HOLLY KRISTIN

Ayurveda Cookbook

https://mybook.to/HollyKristinAyurveda

Pressure Canning Cookbook

https://mybook.to/HollyKristinCanning

Mediterranean Diet Cookbook

https://mybook.to/HollyKristinMedDiet

The Easy AIP Diet Cookbook

https://mybook.to/HollyKristinAIPdiet

Canning & Preserving for Beginners

https://mybook.to/HollyKristinPreserving

The Essential Wood Pellet Smoker and Grill Cookbook

https://getbook.at/woodpelletcookbook

Printed in Great Britain
by Amazon